Towards A Better Life

Towards A Better Life

Anshu Bharti

ZORBA BOOKS

ZORBA BOOKS

Published by Zorba Books, November 2022
Website: www.zorbabooks.com
Email: info@zorbabooks.com
Author Name: ANSHU BHARTI.
Copyright © ANSHU BHARTI.
Title:- Towards A Better Life

Printbook ISBN:- 978-93-95217-14-9
Ebook ISBN:- 978-93-95217-15-6

Zorba Books Pvt. Ltd. (opc)
Sushant Arcade,
Next to Courtyard Marriot,
Sushant Lok 1, Gurgaon – 122009, India

Printed by Thomson Press (India) Ltd.
B-315, Okhla Industrial Area, Phase 1, New Delhi- 110020

Contents

Acknowledgement

I dedicate this book to my parents, Dr. Om Prakash and Mrs. Manorma Prakash who gave me the pluck to face the odds of life with grace and made me capable of sharing my life experiences with people.

I thank my friend Mr. Kalakanhu Panigrahi who had lit a candle for me during my dark days and motivated me to express my feelings once again on paper which I had stopped doing years ago.

My special thanks to my friend Dr. Anirban Pal who helped me assemble my thoughts and put them in the form of a book. Without his support and encouragement, probably this book would not have been in your hands today, dear readers!

I would like to express my gratitude to my online readers who not only showered me with love and blessings but also motivated me to pen down my thoughts in a book - A book that they can cherish for a lifetime.

I am grateful to Mrs. Shalini S Kumar who edited the manuscript in a short time.

Meanwhile, I also convey my heartfelt thanks to Mr. Suresh Menon, a business journalist, for recognising the potential of my writing, for believing in me and guiding me to publish this book.

Last but not least, I am grateful to my 6-year-old son Master Evaan Varshney who observing my sheer desire to become an Author, told me a brilliant thing. He said, "You can become an Author only if you write a book. So don't just speak, write."

Foreword by Dr. Shubha Sreedharan

Anshu Bharti is an enormously gifted writer and I like her writing style. The honesty and unique insight with which she narrates her life experiences and encounters makes this book utterly delightful and readable.

Though there are many incidents and experiences that seem pretty commonplace, what makes them fascinating is the understanding and self-awareness that Anshu demonstrates while dealing with the various problems in her life.

For instance, even while fighting depression and suicidal thoughts, what saves Anshu is her uncompromising attitude. She refuses to be abused and sets limits to the extent to which others can influence her life. Her self-respect and dignity enable her to get out of a toxic relationship and restart her life.

This book is a must-read for every woman who aspires to become strong and independent, and lead a happy and contented life. Anshu's story is sure to inspire a lot of young women struggling to break free from shackles.

The author also dwells on a variety of topics ranging from parenting and divorce to abuse of women and illicit relationships in certain communities. There are also articles on issues that are still conventionally considered taboo, such as sex education for teenagers, love, and sexual relationships. These are discussed with candour and from a refreshing perspective.

Though Anshu often talks about freedom for women, there is no toxic feminism on display. Articles like 'Women are destined to suffer' bring under scrutiny the misogyny prevalent in our society. Even in the darkest of times, Anshu projects optimism and an ability to look for possibilities beyond what is visible to an ordinary mind.

During the Covid-19 pandemic, when people were engulfed in despair about when it would end, Anshu was already planning ahead for trips with her little son once the pandemic dissipated. Given the above, Anshu Bharti could be a trailblazer for many women writers, and her book can be a handy and valuable guide for many readers.

A Letter to Readers

Dear Readers,

When I went through the most difficult phase of my life, I felt as if I was the most miserable soul on this planet, it became my belief that suffering was my destiny. It was the time when I passed through years of intense depression and even contemplated taking my life. I believed there was no power that could rescue me from my situation.

However, there seemed a spirit hidden inside me which wanted to break all the barriers of suffering and blossom. During that time, I somehow started writing on social media platforms. I started venting out my thoughts and views, which helped me comprehend that I was not the only one who was suffering in life. My online readers reached out to me with their tribulations which saddened me more. I realised my pain was lesser than theirs and I felt an urge to help them with my thoughts.

From there, an odyssey began to motivate people to live a life to the fullest. I have written several blogs on various issues that life throws at us from time to time. Readers from all age groups found solace in my writing. They approached me with their personal problems seeking my advice. I tried to help them with my understanding and knowledge as much as I could.

I have received hundreds of 'Thank You' messages for writing my thoughts. The readers find them raw, simple, coming straight from the heart and inspiring. They say they think about me, my stories and thoughts when they feel despondent. Reading my words has become their elixir.

Many of them requested me to write a book which can be helpful to them in the long run. So I have written this book to share with you, dear readers, what I have learnt from my life as well as what I have observed from my surroundings. You can consider it a thought-provoking book which is totally based on my personal experience. I have refrained from preaching anything to the readers like they do in most of the self-help books. Instead, I prefer to guide people to live with grace, through changes that other people I know and I have made in life.

So, I believe this book will never appear to be trying to preach you anything. However, this will show you a path in dark and help you learn how to live with grace as well as self-esteem.

Thank you for reading this book. My constant loving support is always with you.

Love,

Anshu Bharti

The Most Awesome Feeling

When you realize your worth.

When I realised my worth, I stopped wailing over small things. I stopped grousing about my life, instead, I started working on things that I desire for.

The first thing I did after grasping my worth was to walk out of my failed marriage. Yes, without bothering *what people will say.*

I snapped out of suicidal thoughts. I realised, my absence in the world will not impact people who don't care about my emotions. Then why shed tears for them or take the harsh step of ending my life?

Instead, I stood up for myself and started fondling the soul in me that was being hurt for years. If I can't adore myself, how can others?

I completely stopped pleasing people.

Do you know what I do now? I pamper myself. I get ready and go on a date with myself. I talk, laugh and smile alone while driving.

I have never been good at singing. Nowadays, I sing and record it. Then I post it on social media, without bothering *what people will say.*

Sometimes, I dance with my moppet and we laugh together. I try to do exercise and eat healthy every day. I focus on my job because that is the source of my income. I plan to go on trips with my child to experience the world once Covid-19 dissipates.

I spend time interacting with people whom I don't know at all. The best feeling is I am a free soul, answerable to no one.

I maintain a journal to record my thoughts. I spare time to read good books and enhance my wisdom. I try to become kinder every day because we don't know who is going through what. This gives me immense peace.

I want you too, dear readers, to experience this awesome feeling. Come out of the dilemma, insecurities and unnecessary fear. And be a change!

The Boyfriend

When I was in the final year of my graduation, a senior beautifully proposed me. He had watched me every day during the classes. I was a bright student with a zeal to become an independent woman. He liked me and secretly composed beautiful poems and gazals for me.

I had a huge respect for him as he was my senior and also a sincere student.

One day he gifted me a small diary. I thanked him and hastily kept it in my bag. After I returned to my hostel and opened the diary to show my roommate, I was shocked. Half of the diary was full of poems and gazals. His handwriting was like dewdrops. He had beautifully described me in his poems, even my name was mentioned in some of them. They were very deep. He had likened me to a rose, the sunshine, a flowing river and the carelessly blowing wind. Tears rolled down my cheek. The aspiring girl in me melted and the very next day accepted his proposal.

Two of my close friends in the hostel were shocked to know about it.

"How can Anshu fall in love? She is so ambitious and studious." They questioned each other in disbelief.

After my final exams, I shifted to New Delhi for my higher education. My boyfriend stayed in Patna, preparing for civil services. So now, we were in a long-distance relationship and I liked it.

Back in Patna, while in college I never liked the girls in the hostel. They were always busy over the phone, talking to boyfriends. Having lovely talks, fighting and shedding tears did not impress me.

"One should have a purpose in life." I had often thought.

My love story was new. My parents had given me a mobile. I too got busy on calls. My sister called and found the line was busy. My parents too found the line was busy. Every time I felt guilty lying to them. Sometimes, the guilt conscious was so deep that I wept alone as if I was committing a crime.

For me, it was actually a crime. My parents had sent me to study. They were spending money on my studies and here, I was fully occupied keeping myself busy in the games of the heart.

My boyfriend understood my pain. We cut down on our talks and I focused on my studies. Still the guilt consciousness had not subsided. The guilt of telling a lie to the people who had trusted me.

Once he visited Delhi for an exam. After the exam, in the afternoon, we were roaming at India Gate. This is when my brother-in-law who has always loved me like his little daughter called me over the phone and asked me affectionately where I was. I lied to him telling him that I was sitting in my college canteen with my friends. He then said that he had transferred one thousand rupees to my account as a gift and asked me to get a new dress as the festive of Diwali was approaching.

After hearing this, I felt so emotional and errant that I wanted to disappear into the bowels of the earth, just like Sita.

However, I was dedicated to this relationship and wanted to achieve it only after we both got success in our careers. That was the deal.

But, after a few months of the relationship, I found my boyfriend getting possessive. I had to report to him of my daily activities. The love became suffocating when he started controlling me.

"Why did you come in Sameer's car? How many friends were there in the car? You don't know Delhi boys. You are very innocent; you need to be careful." This became a regular dialogue in our calls.

Sameer was my classmate. He had a lovely girlfriend who also studied in our class. He was rich and came to college driving his car. One day, I got to know that he drops his girlfriend and another student on his way back home. They were actually doing carpooling. Sameer was a decent guy. One day, he asked me to join the team. I felt happy as I could travel with him for half of the way and avoid my hectic bus journey.

I joined them. I saved the time, money and exertion that I had been wasting on the bus journey. After returning home, I told my boyfriend about this new arrangement. He got upset. He warned me to not get trapped by such things.

I was shocked. I did not like it. I was inquisitive to know about life and the world. I wanted to explore every bit of it on my own. I had seen babies how they fall, cry and get up again when they learn to walk. I wanted the same for myself. I wanted to experience things - the fall, the hurt and the sense of winning rather than holding someone's hand as support.

My boyfriend could not understand this. I was getting weary of reporting, explaining and defending myself. I felt like being caged. Controlled.

Days started getting gloomy. I cried for my freedom. One night, with a heavy heart, I wrote a poem for myself - My existence wants to expand.

I want to fly,

So high that I touch the sky

Let me take wings

Let me fly around

Let me go beyond

All on my own

Don't teach me how onerous the journey might be

Don't preach to me what precautions I need to take

I don't mind

falling like those autumn leaves

I don't mind

shining like those faded dawning stars

So, let me experience the rise and fall

Let me hunt the space

All on my own

Don't stop me

Don't become an obstacle in my way

I wish to bloom in the sky filled with the yellow sun

I long to possess a realm of it

All on my own

Let me fly

Let me soar high

Because my existence wants to expand.

After a few months, I broke up with him. He was a good soul. His only fault was he was too protective and possessive. He couldn't give me space.

Ruby's Mother

A woman worked as domestic help in my house - Ruby's mother. In small towns and villages, women don't have their own identities. Once they are married, their names are forgotten. They are addressed as someone's wife. If they have children, they are addressed by their eldest child's name.

I recall my school days when I enthusiastically participated in the block and district-level competitions. I collected medals for my speaking skill. People loved listening to my speech. After every speech, the judges asked my teacher about me.

"Who is she?"

"Ah! She is our Doctor Sahab's daughter." The teacher replied.

Everyone knew my father. He is a famous, reputed doctor.

But this irked the little girl in me. I was known as my father's daughter. I did not have my own identity. It was not like I did not love my father. He has always been my hero and I have loved him the most. Still, I have my name and always wanted to be known by my own name.

So this woman's eldest daughter was Ruby. Everyone called her Ruby's mother. Probably, Ruby too never knew her mother's real name. The women in our society are very comfortable with losing their identity. In fact, even educated women happily change their surnames after their marriage and add their husband's names to their last names.

For me, this is not just losing one's name but identity. I never accepted it for myself.

Ruby's mother had four children including Ruby. She was physically very strong. She worked in the fields and in the evenings, she came to help my mother in household chores. She had high self-esteem and really worked hard for a living. Her husband was working in a city and sometimes, sent money for her. But for that money, Ruby's mother had to persuade him by sending him several letters. She was not literate so my mother wrote letters on her behalf.

I remember how she described to my mother what all things should be mentioned in the letters. My mother was good at writing. She added emotions, gratitude and how much the husband was missed by his wife.

After pestering the husband with these letters, she got a few thousand rupees in a year. I could see the smile on her face. She thanked my mother a thousand times.

"I know this is a very small amount. But if I don't pester him to send money, he will spend all on his drinks." She said.

And she was right.

After a few years, her husband came back and settled with her. He was a lazy guy. He started taking his wife for granted. He sat at home all the time and his wife became the breadwinner of the family.

She still worked in the fields and evenings, at my house. My mother always offered food to her. She ate some and carried a portion of it for the children.

Sitting at home all the time, the husband was getting influenced by his eldest brother's wife who never liked Ruby's mother. She provoked him against her.

So one evening, when Ruby's mother reached home, the husband asked her for money. He wanted to buy his drinks. She denied giving. On this, he got furious and beat her with a stick.

The next day, she couldn't go to the fields but came to my mother early in the morning. My mother applied some ointment to her wounds. She cried out of pain.

Gradually, it became a ritual in her house. The husband would beat her with a stick, snatch money from her and accuse her of going out for romancing. The neighbours watched the drama free of cost.

My mother was very sad. She requested my father to scold her husband. My father called him to the clinic and talked to him. I think he shouted at him too. He didn't utter a single word in front of my father. But after returning home, he beat up Ruby's mother suspecting her character, just because my father had supported this woman.

Ruby's mother had huge respect for my father. This blame was just unbearable for her. She had ultimately lost her patience and she became Durga that day. She picked up the same stick and beat the husband.

She changed history. The whole world witnessed how a woman ran after her husband with a stick in hand. Again, free of cost!

If

This 'If' has hindered the growth and evolution of many souls. It has ruined brilliance before that could come into existence.

If I was young, I would have started learning a new language. If I had possessed a beautiful relationship, my life would have been perfect.

If I had time, I would have read many books. If I had a child, I would have never felt lonely.

If I could spare time after job, I would work out.

If I had money, I would have gone for higher studies. If my parents had motivated me enough, I would have done something great in my career.

This 'If' is dangerous. Many miracles could not take place just because of this. So awful, isn't it? We should avoid it as much as we can because it creates unnecessary boundaries around us and makes us feel helpless. We blame our circumstances and surrounding without realising how our laziness and carelessness don't let us grow in life. We have been aimlessly moving on with life, giving lame excuses.

I have seen epipetric plants growing in rocks. They somehow create space for themselves. They are not shackled by 'If'.

I find them quite impressive.

Can a Woman Become a Home-Breaker?

When I started writing about my experiences on social media, I got to interact with numerous people across the world. They found solace in my motivational blogs. I never preached them, I just wrote about my raw experiences and how I emerged from my own miseries in life.

Once I wrote a blog on the topic, "Can a mother-in-law destroy a good marriage?" And my answer was yes, to some extent. There are some women who are too possessive of their sons. They hate to share their son with another woman. In many families, the daughter-in-law really has a hard time coping with this. The sons too find it arduous to maintain a cordial relationship between the mother and the wife.

On this blog, a reader wrote a strange comment, out of context - "A father too can destroy a good marriage".

I did not say anything. The following Sunday I was checking my inbox. I receive many messages from my readers and I have fixed a day - Sunday to reply to those messages. Some messages are full of appreciation, some readers write to me about how my writing changed their life and some write to me about the miseries they are facing.

They ask for guidance. I try to help them on the basis of my personal experience.

So, one Sunday evening, while I was reading the messages sipping my favourite ginger tea with my child playing with his motorbike near me, a message with the headline, "a father too can destroy a good marriage" grabbed my attention. I quickly remembered the comment on my write-up. The reader wrote further in a very polite way, "Respected Mam, I am sorry to bother you. I have been reading you for quite some time and look up to you for your honesty in your writing. I am going through the toughest time of my life and I feel suicidal. Would you like to hear me?"

Reading this, I felt emotional. I immediately responded, "Hi Aman, how can I help you?"

To my surprise, I got a response in a few seconds - "hello Mam, thank you for your message though I had not expected your reply as you must be getting many messages from your readers."

I asked him what was the matter, and why he was feeling suicidal.

"I am 29, a married man with a one-year-old daughter. I had a love marriage. My mother passed away two years ago, hence my father stays with me. I suspect that my wife and my father are in a relationship. I believe they are having an affair. I am unable to take any action as both the culprits are my only family members."

15

"Aman, how can you say such words for your father and wife? You must have misunderstood" I responded with a sense of incredulity.

I belong to a country where the father-in-law plays the role of the father in his daughter-in-law's life and the daughter-in-law holds huge respect for him, probably more than her own father. The relationship between them is considered auspicious. How could I believe Aman's words?

"No Mam, I have observed the changes in my wife. She wears transparent clothes at home. Once I came home at an unusual time and saw them sitting close and eating from one plate. I even noticed my father holding my wife's waist from the back while she was driving the bike and taking him to the hospital for his regular checkups." The reply came.

I was at loss for words. I did not want to sympathize. It might be his misunderstanding too. He had no proper evidence. But I was taken aback by his mental state. He sounded distressed. I advised him to put a CCTV camera in his house if he was capable to do so. He confirmed saying that he is a successful businessman. Money is not a problem.

After 15 days, Aman messaged me again. He told me that he couldn't catch his wife and father doing anything wrong on the camera. I took a sigh of relief. I advised him to consult a marriage counsellor to fix the issues between him and his wife and get the harmony back. He nodded.

I got busy with my daily chores. Forgot Aman's problem believing that he must be leading a peaceful life now.

It was again Sunday. I was going through my readers' messages and found Aman's message. I quickly opened it to read, expecting a thank you message. He must have come out of all his doubts.

He wrote - "Respected Mam, I have lost my zeal to live the life. I am just counting my days. Though I am dying every day, I am unable to commit suicide. I don't want to make my little daughter an orphan.

Sorry to bother you. I confronted my wife and asked her forthright what was going on between her and my father. She confessed to being in a relationship with him. She said that she loved him. Since things are out in the open now, they do things openly. She is no more my wife now, she has taken my mother's place. I can't touch her now as she has been touched by my father. For me, the only option left is - Suicide. I can't stay in the same house. I can't divorce my wife as I can't reveal the reason. I am afraid of losing respect in society."

I had tears in my eyes. I don't know how but I was able to feel the pain he was going through. I immediately gave him my phone number and asked him to talk to me. I never share my phone number on social media for safety reasons but my heart melted after listening to Aman's story. I felt helpless, I couldn't do anything for him. I am neither a counsellor nor a psychologist. Yet I wanted to talk to him.

"Dear Mam, you are very kind. Don't worry about me. I am just counting my days. I will not live long that is for sure. Thank you for listening to me. Please don't share your number with anyone, the world is not a good place. Keep shining, God bless you!" I got another message from Aman.

Tears rolled down. I kept questioning myself if my mother had given me the wrong lesson about a woman's role in a man's life. I had heard her saying that a woman makes the home. But here I saw the exact opposite happening in Aman's life – his wife becoming a home-breaker.

Adding Patriarchal Flavor in the Relationship

My readers feel connected with me and often want to know my opinion. They ask me questions and I answer them based on my personal beliefs and experiences.

Recently, a reader told me that his girlfriend wanted to keep her last name after marriage which he didn't agree with.

The women in India take their husbands' last names as their surnames after marriage. It's common here and no one has an objection. However, I hold a different opinion.

So I replied to him,

I feel proud of your girl.

When I was in school, I was very good at academics. In fact, I was considered the best student in the school.

As a doctor, my father held a very respectful position in the town. He was famous, and known by everyone. So whenever I did something brilliant, people asked, "Whose daughter is she?"

And the teachers used to proudly tell my father's name.

This used to irk me. I loved my father most, but I wanted to be known by my name. That time I convinced myself thinking that I am a small girl. When I grow, I will make my identity like my father and then, people will know me by my name.

Even I decided that I wouldn't be known by my husband's name.

I don't think it should be considered being egoistic. I love my father and I had no competition with my husband, it's just about self-love.

I love my individuality. And there is nothing wrong with that.

I think you should feel proud of your girl who wants to live her life like an emperor, not like a slave. Changing the last name is not going to prove how much she loves you. But if you disagree with her choice, it definitely proves that you will control her freedom in the future. You have no respect for her choices.

Please don't add the patriarchal flavour to the relationship.

A Woman in India

I have a friend. A close friend - Aasif. I know him since my college days. He has always been decent and respectful.

There were days I used to talk to him regularly over the phone. I had just shifted to Bangalore and had no friends here. After reaching home from the office, many a time, I called him and we talked. He was working and staying with friends in Pune at that time. He shared funny stories about his friends. He had a girlfriend and whenever he talked about her, I found him sensible. I admired him and was sure that he will be a great husband in future.

After a few years, I got married. I love my friends and I never want to lose them. So I was still in touch with him. We called each other and spoke whenever time permitted.

After a few years, he too got married and shifted to Bangalore with his wife. His wife Nusrat was a beautiful woman. I once invited them home for lunch. Nusrat was warm and cordial and held a contagious smile. In an hour, we became a team of two sisters. We were together teasing Aasif and pulling his leg. We all had beautiful moments.

While leaving, Nusrat shared her mobile number and expressed her desire to stay in touch with me. I felt delighted with this gesture.

With time, Nusrat got closer to me. She shared all her sentiments with me, even her disappointment with her husband. After a few years, during one of our calls I sensed that she was not happy. There arose many conflicts between the couple and they hardly talked. I advised her not to stop the communication. Communication is an essential element to make the relationship successful. When we lack communication, the charm of the relationship fades away.

Gradually, I got busy in my life and Nusrat in hers. We became mothers and our children became our first priority. We had almost stopped talking.

It was a Sunday afternoon. After a heavy lunch, I wanted to have a siesta. I asked my nanny to take care of the baby and I headed to the bedroom. Suddenly my phone rang, I saw Nusrat was calling me. Almost after 3 years. I felt happy and quickly picked up the call.

We talked for half an hour. She was very upset with Aasif. She was staying with his parents in the village. Aasif frequently visited her. She got four abortions just because Aasif didn't like to take any precautions during intercourse. Every time she conceived, Aasif asked her to visit the government hospital nearby with his younger brother to get it aborted.

Having been brought up in a doctor's family and being a woman myself, I could feel the pain of these unnecessary abortions. Nusrat had become very weak. Staying with in-laws, she had to take care of all the household chores including her two children. She was depressed and needed emotional support. Aasif had no time for this, nor did he bother to take her to the hospital for tubal ligation.

I wondered how a man changes after becoming a husband. I felt sad thinking how a woman in India is still ignored, abused and taken for granted. Do they need to become more vocal, and more aware of their well-being?

Forgive

Forgive for your own mental peace — I grew up hearing this from my parents.

Earlier I did not understand its significance. If I had conflicts with people and I felt hurt, I developed bitter feelings for them. At times, my pain was so intense that I questioned the existence of God.

"Are you really there? Can you punish them for their wrong deeds?" I cried standing before the wooden temple at home.

However, eventually, I realised that forgiveness reduces the pain and constantly cursing the culprits steals the mental peace.

Now I believe the act of forgiveness is absolutely a selfish act. Half of my agony faded away once I learnt to forgive, I learnt to let things go. This taught me the most valuable aspect of life — Acceptance. Yes, I learnt to accept life however it appeared.

And the outcome is so triumphant. I don't complain. I don't blame people who did wrong to me. Instead, I thank them.

Because of them only, I could evolve as a strong person. I got a zeal to motivate people who are suffering in life.

You will find me happy most of the time. *'Who is doing what'* is often none of my business. This helps me stay serene and positive towards life.

The Little Me

I was 6-7 years old. There was some construction work going on in my house. We were staying on the ground floor and the first floor was fully occupied by the mason and his labourers.

The ground floor was newly constructed and we had shifted here after staying for a long time in a joint family. My grandfather was elated as the house was constructed as per his will, near our Shiva Temple. He was a religious person and spent his mornings offering prayers at the temple.

One morning, I was playing on the first floor while the mason was working along with his helpers. They were local people and therefore knew everyone in our family. The mason was talkative and often spoke nonsense. I always disliked him for his red mouth full of betel leaves wrapped with tobacco. Whenever he had to speak, first he had to spit a sufficient portion of it. I hated how he threw out and continued talking and filling his mouth again.

He threw lame jokes and everyone chuckled. Suddenly, he turned towards me and said that he would elope with my mother. In small towns, people build relationships with each other, they don't have to be blood relations to address each other as brother and sister. He hardly talked to my mother but probably considered her as his brother's wife, 'bhabhi'. In our culture, with bhabhi, we have a cordial relationship and often poke fun.

So this mason wanted to tease me by saying such a statement. It triggered me off. I felt offended when everyone giggled at this joke.

"I will break your face if you say this again," I yelled.

Everyone was shocked. They had not expected the little girl to react this harsh. However, I was confident in my action when my mother got to know about this incident and tried to convince me that I should have taken it lightly.

"How could he say such words for you? He must know whom he was talking about." I said to mother.

The Privilege

My parents have never thrust their choices and beliefs on me. They gave their advice but let me make my decisions. They gave me all sorts of freedom. They never stopped me from doing anything. I was free to choose my dress, friends, career and life partner.

Even when I wanted to put a full stop to my failed marriage, they first hesitated but finally supported me wholeheartedly.

I know many men and women who are unable to make decisions. They are restricted by their families, communities and society. They don't know what they have to do with their life. They are always in dark, in dilemma, in uncertainty.

The reason behind this darkness is their upbringing. Their unawareness too. They never enjoyed the taste of freedom.

Let me tell you my parents too are not independent, they too are caged by social dogma. But they never stopped me from thinking beyond. They believed in me and let me move with the flow of life.

Also, I believe, since childhood I have been self-aware. I had this feeling that I should not be controlled. The remote control of my life should be completely in my hand. Maybe, this mindset attracted more independence to my life.

Women are Destined to Suffer

I was going through postpartum depression. My relationship with my husband was going downhill day by day. The more I was seeking emotional support, the more isolated I felt.

The suicidal thoughts were occupying my mind. I started falling sick every now and then. I was torn, both mentally and physically.

Once I fell sick and had become very weak. So I consulted a doctor in Bangalore. She was a young lady doctor. I liked her aura. The way she carried herself was impressive.

The doctor asked me to get some tests done that included blood tests, blood pressure and thyroid tests. She asked me to visit her again with the reports.

I visited her again. The reports were normal, except for my blood pressure. It was too low.

"How are you even walking with such a low blood pressure? Don't you feel giddiness?" She was amazed.

She inquired about other things and reached the conclusion that I don't have any severe health issues.

"Are you stressed? Can I talk to you alone?" She indicated to my husband who was sitting next to me.

My husband left the room. I was afraid and perplexed about what questions she would ask.

"How is your personal life with your husband? Are you happy?" She asked as soon as my husband left the room.

I kept quiet. Tears rolled down my cheeks. She offered me tissue paper.

"Look, if you are not comfortable opening up with me, I will not ask anything personal. As a doctor, I needed to know about your mental state. Anyways, I guess, I can advise you on something. I know many women who are not happy in their married life. Even me. I too have done countless compromises after marriage. Women are born to do compromises. So be happy, you are not alone. Take care of yourself and your health. Avoid taking stress unnecessarily." She advised.

Women are born to do compromises - said by a young, educated woman who was financially independent too. How easily we Indian women have made everything a part of our fate and accepted it as destiny!

I felt clueless as I was not convinced by her approach.

31

Divorce is Beautiful

When I wrote my opinion about divorce on social media a few years ago, I was highly denounced.

"How can one say divorce is beautiful?" The readers were shocked. Hence, they opposed me.

Well, I take divorce easy and wish it could be taken easily by everyone.

I know several couples living in loveless marriages. Arguing, and fighting has become a part of their life. Every day, they go through a bout of internal disarray. Every day they die.

They are depressed. Their souls are dead just because they are not compatible with each other. Also, they have no hope for any improvement in their relationship. But still, they continue. They are bound to continue.

Does it make sense?

I find it absolute nonsense. We are not born to cry, regret or bewail. We are born to be happy in every moment of our life. We are here to live.

But our upbringing is so neurotic, so psychologically sick that it never lets us broaden our thinking. Divorce is still a taboo in our country. A divorced man or woman is not easily accepted in our society. Especially women.

Let me talk about women. Women are always taught to adjust and compromise. They have been considered the goddess of love, sacrifice and patience. Even in the 21st century, they have no courage to walk out of an abusive relationship.

I really wonder. If a marriage is not successful, why are the partners not encouraged to move on? Moving on from a relationship should be very much okay, very much acceptable.

Marriage is just to hold people, to make them prisoners. Divorce is to release them and let them live life how they want.

We need a new mindset. If the partners realize that they are not compatible with each other, separation should be perfectly fine. In these situations, I find a western society more lenient and understanding. They give their people the right to decide for themselves.

But in India, in the name of culture, millions of people have been tortured and forced to live miserable lives. This is absurd. Do we ever think of what the children will learn watching their parents fighting and sobbing? Children observe, they have the capacity to sense everything. They will never be happy seeing their parents unhappy; rather it would be bliss for them seeing their parents be separately happy. They are actually more adaptable than we elders are. So, there would not be a problem here as well.

I ended up with this opinion when I was going through the toughest phase of my life, being in a marriage. The pain was so intense that I was not able to breathe. No one could understand what I was going through. I felt suicidal. One night, I fed my baby and tucked him into bed. I lay down next to him with several negative and positive thoughts in mind.

"Is this how I am going to live all my life?", I asked to myself.

If being in marriage also, I was lonely then what was the use of being in marriage? Why not live alone and have a peaceful life? Divorce is not the end of life but the end of miseries. It must not be considered ugly. It is beautiful.

Self-love vs. Selfishness

Once upon a time, I wanted to feel adequate. I wanted to love myself. I wanted to live for myself.

But how? The moment this question arose in my mind, I felt I was being selfish.

Because my upbringing was like that. I was not taught that self-love is the most important. My upbringing taught me that giving the priority to myself is selfishness.

I wonder how self-love has been misunderstood for ages. A person who sacrifices his wishes and desires for the sake of others is always appreciated. He is called a saint. But in a true sense, a person who first tries to fulfil his wishes is greater. Because he is the one who tastes life first and then, tries to fill the emptiness of others. He is the one who will never cry for anything but can always guide others with his beautiful experiences.

To understand self-love, we need to understand "what can an empty cup pour out?"

If you are yourself inadequate, what can you give to others?

Self-love is a jewel that helps you bloom your personality and lets you spread light around. This is something that fills you in and out. You become overflowing that benefit others too.

The Sign of a Bad Marriage

I was at a party with friends. Some new faces were there whom I had never met before. They were friend's friends. All had come with their spouses.

Drinks and starters were going on. The jokes were being cracked. Everyone was in a fun mood.

Suddenly a child fell down while running. He got hurt in his head. A woman who was nearby lifted the baby in her lap and started calming him down as he was crying loudly.

His parents seemed the least bothered and were engrossed in relishing the food. Maybe, they were used to such hurts and cries and had confidence that things would turn out fine after a while.

However, the baby was still crying loudly.

Suddenly, a loud voice silenced everything. It was the husband of the woman who was trying to calm down the baby. The husband shouted at her as if the fault was hers. He asked her to hand over the baby to his mother, why was she making him cry unnecessarily?

Maybe, he was right. But she was doing it out of love.

I noticed her eyes were filled with tears. She silently gave the child to his mother and pretended to wear a fake smile.

Later I got to know that her husband and child's father were very good friends so he had concerns for the child too.

"So what? How could he yell at his wife in public? Everyone has self-respect. This is not acceptable." I felt agitated with this thought.

In a marriage, one has to respect the other, irrespective of their gender. A couple must maintain each other's respect in public. If it's not vigorously adhered to, the marriage cannot be considered in a good state.

With time, it gets rotten.

The Struggle of My Father

While growing up, my father had faced numerous miseries. He had seen poverty closely though my grandfather had been a landlord under the British rule. He was rich and had abundance in life.

When I asked my father the reason for this sudden poverty, he simply said that time never remained the same for anyone in this world.

I agree. Time changes. Life changes. Nothing is permanent - people, relationships, money, name, fame etc. Anyone can lose anything.

So while growing up, his family had lost everything. They sold their lands whenever they needed money.

My father was in eighth grade when his eldest brother (my uncle) was struggling to give a good life to the whole family. He was wise and was trying his best to bring the lost fortune back. He befriended a doctor in a government hospital.

He invited him to practice in his place. Since the family still held a reputation, the doctor happily accepted the proposal.

My uncle made a small clinic for him where he treated poor people with a nominal amount of 5 Rupees as fee. He bought a second-hand car for travelling. He tried hard to learn to drive but didn't succeed. Later, he kept a driver.

Every day, my father used to observe the doctor. He was a school-going boy, clueless about his career and future. However, he was highly fascinated by the doctor and his profession. He stayed for hours in the clinic after school, observing the doctor. He quickly learnt to inoculate.

One day, a patient came with a painkilling drug that he needed to take through the injection. The doctor had gone out for lunch. My father was sitting alone in the clinic. He convinced the patient and successfully injected him. When the doctor came, he was not able to believe that a 12 year old boy could find the nerve and inject it so well. He was impressed and from there, my father started dreaming of becoming a doctor. My uncle too considered his dreams valuable and encouraged him. Though he did not have money, he sent my father to medical college.

Today, while telling the story to me, my father suddenly started sobbing. The man whom I had known all my life as an extremely reserved person, could open up so well. I wondered. I kept on asking him questions and he kept on satisfying my curiosity. He was absolutely a different man today. Tears in his eyes. Memories of his struggles, dedication and love of his eldest brother for him in his heart. To me, he was an inspiration.

"I went to a medical college to become a doctor, but I had no money to survive. I woke up early and gave tuition to children every day before I went to college. Then again in the evening, I taught children. I studied all night and often fell asleep over the books" He said.

He was very good at teaching and was soon referred by people for teaching. He was later paid 50 Rupees per student. This helped him manage his college fee and two meals.

"Every day I had only one meal that I had learnt to prepare - khichdi. I was frustrated eating the same thing. Once I was cooking khichdi and was crying, suddenly my brother arrived to see me. He saw me in tears. He didn't say anything and left. After 15 days, he found someone to be my roommate. The roommate was from our village and had come to work in the city. The deal was that he wouldn't pay the room- rent but would cook for me. The days became slightly better in terms of food." My father said with a smile.

However, the struggle to become a doctor did not get over. It continued until he became a doctor in the year 1974 and started his own clinic in his hometown.

He established his clinic in the same place where the doctor, his inspiration, had treated the patients. He had kept his name written on the wall intact until the last year. He told me the clinic's walls were painted in his absence the last year, and they painted over the name. I could sense his sadness while telling me this.

Most Important Thing I learned in Life

No matter how good you are you will be judged.

I personally know many people who are true, genuine and have never done anything wrong to anyone. Still, there are SOME people against them, denouncing them.

These SOME people will be always there in everyone's life. Look at the history.

In Ramayana, Rama was known for his perfection. Sita was admired for her chastity. Still, they had critics and had to go through a lot.

Mahatma Gandhi was adored by the mass but had critics too. And one day, he was even killed by one of his haters.

These are just a few examples. If you look around, you will wonder how people judge others and deprecate. They don't miss any chance to label others as failure, characterless, fake.

You never know how you are perceived by others. Society is always there to put you in the dock.

So the most important thing that I have learned in life is being myself. I don't pay heed to others' perceptions. I do what I feel is correct. I learned that I don't have to bother about the society and its stereotypes. In the last two years, I have become dumb and deaf. I don't hear what others say about me and I don't react if I ever accidentally hear them. I have maintained a distance from everyone who doesn't seem to understand me. I can't afford to waste my time in giving an explanation to them. My time and energy are very precious to me.

I have got one life that too holds so many uncertainties. I don't know when it will be over. Then why bother others? And who the hell they are to make the rules of my life???

So in a nutshell, I don't give a fuck to judgemental opinions and perceptions of people. I did, I do and I will do what I like to do. Simple!

Here I recall a poem that I had written in this context:

Make your own world
Live your life,
Take your sword-
Fight your battle
After all, it's your life!

Be in the crowd,
but listen to your heart.

Let them follow what they want-
but you walk your own path.
After all, it's your life!

Love your surroundings-
A dewdrop, a flower, a human, though
make sure you are not obsessed.
Accept your aloneness.
After all, it's your life!

Everyone is in a race-
By competing with them don't create a mess,
Be yourself,
Be at your own pace.
After all, it's your life!

You have your thoughts-
your own opinion.
Though the army of fools is around,
you don't let them dictate,
don't let them rule.
After all, it's your life!

Giving Space is as Important as Breathing

I was sitting in a cafe.

A couple came arguing. The man was furious that the woman didn't listen to him. I heard the woman saying she didn't listen because he often preached to her. (The song, "Papa, don't preach...." immediately came to my mind.)

However, the man said defending himself he always wanted to assure her safety. He loved her so much.

"Don't do this, don't do that. You must go this way, not that way." This is how we suffocate the life of our loved ones. We think we are protecting them. But as a matter of fact, we make them handicap.

We don't understand that we have no authority to control others' life. We can show the path but we cannot force them to choose the same. Something may be right to you but wrong to others.

I have seen most parents doing the same to their children. Once I asked a child what he wanted to become in life.

"Pilot", He said beaming.

"Why do you want to become a pilot?"

"I don't know. Mumma says I want to become a pilot." He replied rolling his eyes.

That 5-year-old boy left me awestruck. He was yet to see the world. He was yet to taste life. But he knew what he had to become.

Everyone has their own individuality. Their own uniqueness. If we are not able to find it, it's our fault. We cannot mold people as per our choice. We are no one to decide things for them. We must know it.

Giving space is the most important thing anyone can do for their loved ones.

Persistence

My baby had an abscess in his throat. His face got swollen - it became just double his original face. It started slowly and he was in severe pain for the next 10 days.

My uncle, who is one of the best homoeopathic doctors in North India, has been treating him since 2020 when he was diagnosed with adenoids. The doctors in Bangalore had asked me to immediately go for an operation, as it was too critical.

"Immediately means?" I asked the doctor with tears in my eyes.

"Within 3-4 days", he clarified.

I felt clueless. I was at one of the most reputed hospitals in Bangalore. I had to believe his words. I asked him if there was any risk in the operation.

"The bleeding doesn't stop sometimes and this is when the situation gets critical", the doctor was too candid and blunt.

I was sobbing in the hospital thinking how much the universe will still test my patience.

This was the time my uncle came into the picture and took the responsibility to cure him with homoeopathy. Under his observation, my baby became alright and now, there is no need for the surgery.

So I trust him a lot.

This time, when he had an abscess in the throat and was in bed for 10 long days, without eating proper food, my family, staying miles away, was losing patience. They insisted on visiting a physician who will operate and remove the abscess. But I had a different mindset. I could not get myself to have faith on the doctors here.

My sister became so impatient that she wanted to send my brother-in-law to take care of the baby.

But I was persistent. I knew my uncle will heal him but it will take time. However, I often cried looking at him.

The medicine worked slowly and when the abscess was about to come out, I had to burst it and clean it. That was the toughest job as I had never done it before and was scared too. The baby was in too much pain and was not allowing me to do.

But I did it - crying and screaming.

I felt a mother has a huge potential. She can become Shakti and nurture her child even in odd circumstances.

I fear problems but at the same time, I try to keep my spirits up. I believe we cannot run away from problems, so it's in vain to imagine a life without them.

My sister and brother-in-law are always ready to come to Bangalore whenever I face such challenges. But I asked them to wait, not to rush. As a single mother, my journey has just started. Such problems will keep coming. So I believe I need to be audacious enough to face them, instead of calling people every now and then.

I am grateful to my family and friends to be always there for me, but I can't depend on them for every single thing. I think this is what makes me, ME.

Think Negative

Think negative for a few minutes every day.

My father is 74 years old. He is a doctor who has always been into yoga and lived a healthy lifestyle.

However, due to age, he has now become a little cranky and sometimes, unnecessarily takes out his irritation on my mother.

Once he was being cranky and was getting annoyed with us, I asked him to think negative.

"Why should I think negative? Everyone recommends thinking positive and you are asking me to think negative." He frowned.

"Yes, think negative. Imagine that your wife is not there, who will cook for you? Imagine that you don't have a good relationship with me. You say something and I get angry at you. How would you feel?"

He listened to me patiently.

"Imagine that you are unable to walk. You are so emaciated that you can't even go to the washroom on your own. How helpless you would feel!" I continued.

He didn't say anything and understood my point.

In our day-to-day life, we are only advised to think positive. Nobody tells us the importance of negative thinking. By thinking negative you realise the importance of your surroundings. You feel grateful, instead of complaining and becoming sad.

Many a time, when people pity me by pointing out my single life, my heart sinks. I then immediately remember my days when I was stuck in a relationship and felt wretched. Being alone is better than being with someone with whom there is no peace.

We often blame the current situation and never try to think that the current situation is actually better than something unpleasant that could happen to us.

Hence, I advise you to think negative for a while every day, if you want to live life in abundance.

The Scariest Situation

In the year 2006 — I had recently shifted to Delhi for my education. It was my first winter over there.

I had early morning classes for which I started at 6:30 am every day. One morning, I was at the bus stop, waiting for my bus.

It was a foggy morning. Too cold.

I felt my uncovered palms freezing.

My bus was late for its usual time. I was alone at the bus stop and even the road was deserted.

Suddenly a middle-aged man came to the bus stop, dressed in a jogging suit. He stood quiet for a while and then started murmuring something weird.

I felt scared as soon as my sixth sense sent danger signals to my mind. I started walking away from there, and to my surprise, he too started walking behind me.

I paced up towards the next bus stop which was two kilometers away from there. He too did the same. He was still murmuring dirty words though I couldn't make out what exactly he was speaking.

There was no one around to whom I could call for help. After a few steps, I turned behind and found him chasing me.

The fear had engulfed me.

I started running and so did he. After running 500 meters, I had no guts to look behind and check if he was still there. I kept running until I reached the next bus stop.

I was gasping and sweating. To my relief, there were some people at this bus stop and when I looked behind, that stalker was also not there.

Now, I burst into tears, without bothering about my surrounding.

After six years, on 16th Dec 2012, when the Nirbhaya case took place in Delhi, I was living in Bangalore. This incident disturbed me a lot. The girl was brutally raped and murdered. I could see myself in her. I could feel her pain in my body. I had become indifferent. My colleagues in office asked me why I was cold and frigid. I could not tell them that I too could have become Nirbhaya a few years ago.

We are living in a country where we fight for years to hang a rapist. Even if the crime is proven, justice is not in the bag. The women are not safe here. Their safety is not guaranteed even in public places.

Role Model

Years ago, I was attending a seminar where they had asked me about my role model.

And I was stuck. I didn't know whom to mention as my role model.

I still don't have any specific role model.

Sometimes I feel my mother is my role model who has stood like a rock to face all the difficulties with huge patience. My father is just a saint on this earth. To be honest, I have not seen another selfless person like him. I have lots to absorb from him as well.

I liked a clerk in my college with whom I used to spend time during my breaks. She had left her alcoholic husband and was singlehandedly bringing up two children. Somehow, she had managed to get this job in the college and was content, however, I could not help notice her wet eyes while we talked.

I liked a friend who had faced poverty and struggled to get even a single meal in childhood. And now, he is successful in his career. I admire him a lot.

My aunt had lost her teenage son and went through severe depression for several years. She was not able to do her daily chores, and hardly recognised anyone. We had lost hope that she will ever recuperate. But she has bounced back and is normal now.

I see so many people around me whom I feel like considering a real hero. I don't have any specific person. But there are countless people in this world and knowing their personal stories, I get inspired and make a decision not to give up on life.

It's okay if you don't have a role model. Why do we need a role model when there are countless people around to inspire us?

I don't have any role model. I just look for an opportunity to find someone who can motivate me to proceed with life however it appears.

A Thought from My Diary

It is 12:50 am. I am awake. Tried hard to sleep but couldn't. Beside me, my child is in deep sleep. His face is glowing pink in the beam of light coming in through the window. And here, my heart is fantasizing many things about him.

I feel sorry looking at children who are so pressurized to achieve 90% marks. It irks me when I listen to parents how they dream about their children's success in this materialistic world. They never teach them how to face failure which is also an essential part of life.

I don't want my child to be in the rat race. I don't want to teach him to be a part of the crowd. Instead, he should learn to be himself. I want him to discover life beyond this worldly affair. He should equally be aware of success and failure.

I will tell him it's okay if he is not good at mathematics or if he is not able to grasp a particular subject. There have been many people who have scored poor marks, but still they could climb the ladder of success. Maybe it was absolutely a different field, such as music, dance, sports, swimming or writing.

He doesn't have to feel bad if his fellow student is better at something. The world doesn't end there. He needs to develop another skill.

I will tell him it is not necessary to become a doctor or engineer for being happy. Happiness is within you. You just have to find it. You just have to be yourself. Because success is doing things that you like.

You don't have to follow things because your mother has followed them. You must learn to analyse things on your own and reach the conclusion.

It's your life. Life is the only gift you have received and you can claim it to be yours. Don't misuse it. Don't waste it. Take the opportunity to use it for others as well. Be a good human and accept humanity as the best religion.

Hope, my wishes come true.

How Do I Have an Easy Life?

Years ago, I was travelling on a train with my brother-in-law. We didn't get the reservation, so we got onto a local train.

I am not used to the crowd (not even my brother-in-law) and also, was quite uncomfortable that the train stopped at every small station. The three hours journey seemed too long.

I was getting restless. On the other hand, my brother-in-law was cool and fully occupied in reading the newspaper that he had snapped up before boarding the train. This irked me more.

When I shared my frustration with him, he smiled and advised me to take this journey as an opportunity to have a good, long sleep.

And to my astonishment, after a few minutes, he dozed off. Throughout the journey, he was either sleeping or reading the newspaper.

That day, I realized that life is tough but we make it tougher by not accepting it. We overthink, panic and feel dismayed.

So, learn to accept life however it comes. It will become easy.

You are going through a tough time in life. Everything seems to be falling apart. If you can fix it, fix it. Else accept it. Don't bewail.

You are seeking a solution to a problem but not getting anywhere. Then understand that it is probably not a problem to be solved but rather a truth to be accepted.

You have lost your job, loved ones, or bank balance. Don't panic. There is always a way to move on. Find it out.

People whom you loved the most have changed. They turned their face away when you needed them. Don't grumble. They were never yours. Accept it.

Accept your disease, depression, sleepless nights, loneliness and miseries. Sometimes, a few things need to be accepted. They need to be left unbothered. Because they are hard to change. But remember, there is always a way to move on.

Moreover, the day you learn to find an opportunity even in miseries, life will be easier for you. No matter how bad the circumstances are, you will have something beautiful around you. You just need to have the ability to see that beauty.

Addiction

"Do you have an addiction to anything?" The colleague asked me.

"No. I am not addicted to anything." I replied.

But deep down, I know I have an addiction. I am addicted to myself. I am so much in love with myself that I don't mind calling it an addiction. I love my aloneness. I love my being. I wish to enhance it every day.

There were days when I wanted to become like somebody. Like my parents, like my teacher, like Kiran Bedi, like Indira Gandhi.

I was in the race. In fact, I had always been in the race. I wanted to become studious like my next-door neighbour's son, I wanted to sing like my sister. This longingness was never-ending. I was so involved in the process of being somebody else that I never looked into myself. I never knew what I was. I never knew my existence. Always in the race, no time to discover the actual me.

But gradually, slowly and slowly I started discovering myself. From one page to another, from one chapter to another,

I started navigating. I realized that there was a lot of potential to be discovered.

I took time, in fact, I am still in the process to know myself, to be myself. Now, I am neither nobody nor somebody. I am me, very much me.

We often inspire our children to become like someone. We never teach them to be themselves. Score 90% marks how the neighbour's son did, do this and do that how others are doing. They start imitating and the results are in front of you - more suicidal cases, more frustrated people. If some of them become doctors and engineers also, they don't remain original. All are wearing a mask.

Our system, teaching and training are so baseless, so neurotic. It is making everyone mad.

Everyone is talking about others, nobody is talking about himself or herself. This is so foolish.

We need to train our children to be themselves.

I know a writer who is not earning much. But he is a happy, content soul because he is working on his passion. He is being himself.

Your happiness, your contentment, what else is required in life?

Living Alone

In the last few years, there have been many people who have preferred to live single throughout their life. In a country, like India, living alone is still a big deal. Such people are often not accepted by our society. They are even demeaned and belittled.

I believe living alone is underrated.

"If you stay single, you will be left alone. Nobody will be there with whom you can share your emotions. Especially, in your old age, loneliness would be unbearable. There would be no one to care for you."

This is what we hear about living alone.

But if you are independent enough, I mean mentally, living alone is a blessing. You can do whatever you like. You can arrange your house as you wish. You can design your bedroom however you like. You find your things exactly where you kept them.

You have no one to take you for granted, and neither you do this crime with anyone. Once you are full of your aloneness, you crave togetherness. You become kind and love to have people around you.

By living alone, you learn things like cooking, managing, arranging and making decisions. You become conscious and careful. You don't take risks with your health. You start taking care of yourself.

Society has given many wrong messages based on which we have developed our mindset. Living alone is one of them.

Living alone doesn't mean that you will be living in a desert and you will have no one in your life. You can definitely call your loved ones to your home and celebrate. You can enjoy life with people with whom you are compatible.

When I decided to extricate myself from the miseries of my failed marriage, many people including my family had only one concern about how I would live alone.

"You are so young. How would you live such a long life alone? Being a woman, you need someone to lead your life."

Still, I am often asked by my relatives if I have thought of remarriage or not.

Listening to everyone, I ask myself if I am afraid of being alone and every time the answer I get is a big NO.

Aloneness has never frightened me. In fact, I feel complete, composed and more confident in my aloneness. I don't have to give an explanation to anyone for things that I do and at the same time, I don't look for an explanation from anyone for things that they do. This way I am able to save a lot of my time and energy and utilise them for things that I love to do. My aloneness is a boon to me. This has helped me escape from emotional turmoil. Whenever I recall my past, I feel grateful to have reached this wonderful stage.

My mother often says we are all children of the universe. The universe only gives us food and shelter but we are often misguided to not believe that. We think that we get food at the mercy of our parents, spouse, employers etc.

That's completely wrong. We are just the creatures on this earth run by the universe. Aloneness or togetherness doesn't add happiness to life. It's only you who enrich yourself.

There is no need to get afraid of being alone.

The moment you embrace this thought, you will overcome the fear of being alone. So far in my life, I have lived alone, fought alone. Sometimes I won, other times I lost. But the most content feeling I have is I did not let anyone ruin my life just because of my emotional dependency.

Can We Live Natural?

Once I attended a workshop where I met this wonderful man. After the event got over, together we had coffee over a beautiful talk. He told me he has a big heart full of emotions. He wants to express them. He wants to cry his heart out when he feels low. But he doesn't.

"What stops you?" I asked.

"Society. It says men should not cry." He said and we had a good laugh.

But deep down, we knew it was not a joke. Society has conditioned us in such a way that we can not live life in its original form. It asks us to go against nature.

We often hear - Shedding tears fall under the girls' department. I wonder if emotions are also gender-based. How can we question our emotions? How can we expect them to be controlled in one gender, and flow in another? This is absurd because a man has as many tear-glands in his eyes as a woman. It means even nature meant him to cry and weep in the time of grief.

I had read an incident about Obama who cried in public while discussing gun violence in the U.S. Feeling emotional or crying doesn't diminish the power or respect for men but it shows their compassion and caring nature.

There are many, many myths that society has burdened us with. I wish someday we could live as natural as we are.

The Idea of Feminism

I don't like the idea of feminism. I believe that women don't have to fight with men to prove themselves equal to them. Equality is something that has to be earned. Being aggressive against men will take them nowhere.

They are no less than men. They are power. They are a strength. The only thing that they need to do is to collect all the atoms into a form and become a potential. They need to realize their intelligence. They need to become fully aware of the fact that they have the capability to create and recreate.

They can be a doctor, engineer, musician, dancer or pilot.

But in the past, they had been taught that they were born only to reproduce the children. Their only job was to take care of the family. I don't criticize it, nor underestimate the art of reproduction. But now the time has changed. The earth is overpopulated. The world has more people than it requires.

We don't need any more people.

Hence, I have a very different opinion now. I strongly feel women should not invest their energy in reproduction. Women who are not willing to have children must be encouraged/appreciated.

And then, the women should invest their energy into creating something else.

They need to focus on themselves now. They should become a writer, doctor, professor, painter whatever they want.

In this way, not only will they be able to conquer the world, but also they will create beautiful humankind.

The women must think over it because crying, whining never helps. These acts only make them miserable. So I ask them to be thoughtful. To be graceful.

And to break the stereotypes.

Acceptance vs Gratitude

I have done many compromises in life as it did not go as per my plan — from my career to my personal life and from being myself to being with people.

At times, I felt miserable but I always focused on things that I had, instead of that I didn't. If I failed to have a successful marriage, I concentrated on my child and other family members who were always there to love me.

I believe in the law of attraction and try to think positive as much as I can. I repeat to myself what I want in life, with a smile on my face.

I don't know how much it works. But I have developed this faith after reading a few books.

Some people in my neighbourhood unnecessarily poke their noses and try to trouble me. I argued with them initially but later gave up, consoling myself that they are mud. If I throw stones in the mud, it will only spoil my clothes.

"Let's not fight with fools." my child has even started saying this.

I strongly believe there is nothing permanent in the universe. Things change, the situation changes. It's futile to bewail. After every dark night, there's a brighter day. This belief consoles me during my gloomy days.

I have learnt to accept. Things that I can't control or change, I accept. I don't make noise.

From time to time, I make a list of things that I am grateful for. This calms me down, in fact, makes me feel abundant.

Feelings Never Perish

I once fell sick and got admitted to the hospital. There, I met this elderly woman in her 70s. She had fractured her hand and her bed was just next to mine.

She was bright and beautiful. She carried a charm that fascinated me and I was drawn towards her to know her as a person. I often talked to her whenever I felt a little better. In two days, we got closer and she opened up to me.

"I find a friend in you, Anshu." She said while eating her lunch.

She loved music and told me she was fond of old Bollywood songs and found solace listening to them.

She was a graduate. During her college days, she fell in love with her classmate.

"We were made for each other. We shared the same philosophy about life. If I was married to him, I would have been the luckiest girl in this universe." She sounded like a cute young girl while telling this.

However, I noticed a drop of tear in the corner of her eyes.

"Why didn't you marry him?" I couldn't resist asking.

"Our families didn't agree to the inter-caste marriage and we gave up." She said with a fake smile.

"Where is he now?" I asked.

"He lives in Assam. He is a doctor. After my graduation, I married a businessman from an affluent family. It was an arranged marriage and everyone in my family was happy with this knot, except me. However, with time, I accepted my husband and his family wholeheartedly, considering it my destiny. I got busy with my new life and didn't look back." She sadly narrated.

"Were you happy in your marriage?" My curiosity was at its peak.

"I never got time to think about it. Had three children within a few years of my marriage. My husband was always on business trips, and could hardly manage time for family. Taking care of three children alone kept me occupied until they got their own wings. Now, they are settled in the USA and I have lots of time to analyse my past. Love never dies you know." She said with her eyes closed.

I could sense the emptiness that this woman has been carrying in her heart for years. And the immortal feeling - love never dies!

I felt emotional.

"What if she had got married to the love of her life, how satisfactory life would had been!" I kept on thinking.

In our country, we are so obsessed with religion, caste etc that we don't mind killing beautiful, tender souls before they blossom.

A Story that Changed My Way of Thinking

I had been constantly hurting myself with these questions:

Why do bad people always do wrong and still, enjoy their life? Why do good people never take revenge, but keep forgiving them?

I was becoming restless as I was not getting the answer from anywhere.

And then, my mother called me and told me this story:

There was a saint sitting on the bank of a river. A scorpion nearby was trying to drink water but it slipped and fell into the river. It was struggling to come out. The saint felt sad looking at it. He wanted to help.

He tried to pick it up. But every time he tried, the scorpion stung his finger. And in pain, he screamed. However, he didn't stop putting his efforts to rescue it from the water.

The drama went on for several minutes. A man was watching it from far and wondering if the saint was insane.

"My Lord! The scorpion is going to sting you every time you try to save it. Why don't you give up and let it drown?" The man asked the saint.

"My dear child, the scorpion is not stinging me intentionally. It's his nature. Just as it is the nature of water to make me wet. So it's the scorpion's nature to sting, my nature is to save. Why should I leave my nature?" The saint replied.

"So bad people do wrong or speak ill because it is their nature. They are unable to realize what they are doing. But good people can't think of doing wrong as it is not in their nature. They can only forgive and move on." My mother ended her story with this.

And I took a sigh of relief and felt at peace.

Nothing is Permanent

Once I was going through a hard time.

I was feeling low and depressed. I hated gatherings. I hated attending the calls. I was not able to share my despair with anyone.

I was quiet.

But somewhere, I was at peace.

Why?

Because I was being myself. I was keeping everything to myself.

I got more time to spend alone and analyse the things which were for or against me.

I knew sharing with someone may lighten me up but it would be temporary. It won't reduce my pain. Also, it might be risky. I might be mocked by others as this world is full of mockers.

Then why share?

I sat alone. I passed my time alone. I believed everything was about the time that had to pass.

"Time is powerful." My mother often says.

I became more patient. I learned to be calm and serene. Waited for the right time to come as I believed nothing was permanent. Neither good phase nor bad phase.

And my belief worked not because something miraculous happened but because the scars faded with time. I entered into a new phase of life where the new things kept me occupied. I started seeking positivity from them as they were completely different from the previous situation. This helped me evolve stronger than I was earlier.

I would like to share a beautiful quote from Bhagawad Gita here,

"Little by little, through patience and repeated efforts, the mind will be in your control. Doing your work sincerely and removing the expectations will make you live peacefully. Do what you love or else love what you are doing."

Maintenance

The year 2009, is when I started working. And in the span of a year, I had enough savings to get a new bike.

It was so beautiful, so close to my heart. I named it Eliza Doolittle (on the name of my favourite character from Bernard Shaw's novel 'Pygmalion').

I adored it. Cared for it. I never forgot the date when it had to go for the service.

The first few years were full of care and love. But gradually, I started becoming careless. Whatever the reason was, I got married, had a baby and had lots of issues in life that I could not pay attention to Eliza.

It suffered. Or I should confess, I made it suffer.

Engine oil was getting over, still I was driving. Sometimes it stopped, the other time it felt my pain and pushed itself to reach the destination.

I was always late to the service center. Eliza started giving me warnings. Self-starter, engine, the carburetor was threatening me from time to time.

Still, I failed to take its proper care. One day, Eliza was so full of neglect that it revolted and denied moving in the middle of the way. I had to pull it with all my strength to the mechanic's shop. Ah! That was terrible. Later, it costed almost 10k. It got repaired now but the trust is gone.

Why am I sharing this here?

I see many families where people start taking their loved ones for granted. They don't care about each other. They simply don't take heed. The family becomes just a group of people because love is missing there.

Their togetherness doesn't consist of affection and care. It is just because of dependency.

You know everything/everyone needs maintenance. Else they become rusty. With time, they lose their charm.

You need to spend your time and energy on relationships, else either they would become cold or revolutionary. The promises you make at the beginning of your relationship must be renewed and updated from time to time.

Maintenance is the keyword for the day. Don't forget it.

Nothing is Ugly

I was at a family function. A 14 year old girl got her menstrual cycle. I believe it began before the expected date. She was not prepared.

I could sense a sudden surge of nervousness in her body language. I found some stain on her skirt and so guided her towards the washroom. On the way she was hiding as if she had committed a crime.

I asked why she was so uncomfortable. She told that this is an ugly thing. Her mother told her we women should hide it from men.

"There is nothing ugly in this world, Jani," I said in a firm voice.

I strongly feel that it is high time to avoid such misconception. Our men are more understanding these days. Menstruation is not unholy and loathsome. There is nothing irreligious here. So there is nothing to hide.

When I told my opinion to that little girl, she was amazed.

"I will tell your words to my mother, Anshu didi".

I nodded with a smile.

I gave her a sanitary napkin from my bag and she headed to the washroom. Yes, this time with confidence and a wonderful smile.

My son learned about menstruation when he was four years old. When he asked me about the sanitary napkins that he saw in our cupboard, I did not hide the truth from him. I told him in a simple language that I bleed once in a while and I use it as my diaper. He felt concerned and since then, he became caring towards me during my period. He is six years old now and understands that his mother feels weak during this time. He should not trouble her.

Time has really changed. We are living in the 21st century and we are in need of sex education. Our young generation (irrespective of their gender) must be taught about menstruation, sex, condoms etc. Those days are gone when things were kept hidden. Now, it's time to wipe out the old beliefs and make our children more comfortable with life.

An Excerpt from My Diary

I see many young mothers, complaining that they have lost their 'Me-time', due to their child. They feel restricted and saddled with an onerous responsibility.

But today, I realized how excruciating it feels, to be childless.

My father is a doctor. He mainly deals with the female reproductive system. Women, who could not conceive, even for 10–13 years, take treatment from him and are blessed with a child.

He keeps receiving thank-you calls. This is quite normal for us. But today, while having breakfast, a couple called from Delhi, and the woman was literally crying over the phone. My dad was consoling them, his eyes were moist. The tears of happiness!

After the call, dad told me that the couple had been trying for a baby, for nearly nine years. They took treatment from everywhere, with no result. They were losing hope and were about to give up when they came to know about dad. They visited him and took the treatment. After two months of medications, the woman conceived.

She was crying out of joy. She wanted to touch my father's feet. When he prescribed some medicines over the phone, for continuation, she refused to buy from her place. She confirmed his availability and told him that she would come to take it from his hands.

This mixed feeling of faith, trust, joy and emotions melted my heart today.

I straight away headed to the bedroom, my child was in a deep sleep. I kissed him gently and thanked the Almighty for this beautiful gift.

I don't know why I am feeling emotional while writing this. Dad receives countless thank you cards, postcards and calls. Are they just a thank you expression? Or, do they hold deep emotions inside?

When I looked into the sparkling eyes of that old man, I found them as deep as the emotions, inside those cards.

Compassion

I was 10-11 years old. My grandfather was in his late 80s. He had begun to have memory lapses and had started losing his mind. He walked with the help of crutches.

But still, he was very disciplined and health-conscious. My mother made sure that everything arranged for him, was perfect. Lukewarm water for the bath, food properly cooked and boiled, medicines, milk, fruits and his Ayurvedic powders - everything should be perfectly placed.

One day, he was sitting in his room.

A fruit vendor came calling my mom. Our hometown is a small place, so she used to buy fruits and vegetables in bulk and store them in the fridge for the next few days.

The cost was a little high, so she was bargaining. Grandfather was listening to everything from his room. I was doing my homework on the veranda.

Suddenly, he came out fuming. He shouted at the vendor for keeping the prices high. Then he started scolding my mother.

"What sort of a woman are you? Day and night my son works so hard and you waste his money like this. Let him come home today, I will tell him how you are dissipating his hard work."

Mom kept quiet and to my surprise, she was simply smiling. She paid the money to the vendor and went back inside.

Later, in the evening when she was cutting an apple into thin slices for the grandfather, I asked why didn't she tell him that time that he too eats the fruits?

She grinned.

"Again you are smiling. Are you crazy, mom?" I asked in disbelief.

"Because he didn't shout at me. He was simply taking out his frustration. Old people do that and knowing this, I certainly shall not shirk my duty" She answered.

"Whoa! This is ultimate." I murmured to myself.

"Did you say anything?" She asked.

"Nah!" I left considering it was none of my business.

The best thing I have always observed in my mother is her compassion towards elderly people. She is realistic and believes that everyone is in line. She will also reach that stage where she may lose her mind or may become fragile and depend on others.

I have seen her taking care of other elderly relatives from my father's side - without complaining. They too felt comfortable staying in our house, I think the reason was my mother's openness. She embraced people.

I would have been 7-8. An old man working at my place was very affectionate towards my mother. We called him - Huro baba. He had worked for our family as a domestic help for a long time. As he became weedy, he left working in our house. Still, he often visited my mother. She used to lovingly take him to the kitchen and make him sit on a stool. Then she offered him food and a cup of tea. Sometimes, she packed some snacks for him and he baled them in the towel that he always carried on his shoulder.

In return, he showered his blessings on her. The whole scene was heart-touching.

Now, I wish I could see the same compassion and affection in today's families. I feel grateful to my mother who has unknowingly instilled good morals and values into me. Looking at her, I too have developed a soft corner for old people.

Parenting is an Art

Two years ago, I was at Supermarket with my 4 year old son. We were shopping.

"Mumma… I want this. Please." He asked me for an elegant-looking toy car.

I got scared as I guessed the price.

I knew he was becoming a little adamant. Saying 'No' would be a big challenge for me. Probably all the customers and cashiers would gather around us.

This thought alone terrified me.

"Oh god! Please help me." I murmured to myself.

I checked the price. I was right. It was 1,975 INR.

I was already tired of his countless toys. They had alone eaten a good share of my salary. So I decided to control it now on.

"Okay! Once you decide to fight a battle, don't look back." I consoled myself.

"Sweetheart! Listen to Mumma. This car is very costl…."

"Nooooooo, I want this." He screamed without me completing my words.

"Okay, I will buy it for you. But for this, we need a lot of money that Mumma doesn't have right now."

He looked perplexed by this contradictory statement.

I quickly picked up a piggy bank which was lying at the other corner.

"Baby! Let's buy this first."

"What is this?" He rolled his eyes.

"This is a piggy bank. Every day I will come from the office and give you money. You will put that money in this" I said showing him the hole.

"What will happen then?" He was unable to relate.

"Then one day, you will save a lot of money in this. With that money, we will buy this costly car."

"Wow! Nice idea. Mumma, come, let's buy this first." He pulled me towards the billing counter.

I heaved a sigh of relief.

Parenting is an art. I am gradually learning it.

I would like to mention a recent example.

He is six now. He is good at studies. In fact, he is more intelligent than children of his age. I get positive feedback from his teachers.

However, this intelligence didn't come to him just like that. My constant efforts to teach him regularly plays a vital role.

But at times, it becomes difficult for me to manage my work with his studies. As a working mother, I don't get enough time to sit with him and teach him.

It becomes more complicated when he turns undisciplined and disobedient. I keep running behind him and after multiple follow-ups, he writes just one page. And sometimes he is too adamant to listen to me.

So, one such evening when he was not listening to me, I announced that I wouldn't be buying anything that he wanted. I wouldn't be preparing his favourite food. No more online games. And even that he has to sleep without me.

He was shocked by this announcement. He cried too.

I then asked him to clap.

"Clap using only one hand," I said.

He looked at me in disbelief.

"Yes, clap," I reiterated.

He shook one hand in the air and asked,

"How is it possible?"

"Yes, it is not possible. You cannot clap with one hand. Likewise, you cannot get things without paying anything. If

I fulfil all your wishes, you too need to listen to me. We need to work as a team." I was quite stern while stating this.

He understood the rule.

Sometimes, we parents need to be forthright with our children to keep them on track.

Four Days at the Hospital

Due to my father's health issues, I was at the hospital for four days.

In four days, I felt connected to so many people.

Every time, I saw the next-door bedridden patient, we exchanged smiles. He was an old man and his caretaker was also of his age. Once I went to him and told him he would be alright soon. He gave me a big smile and blessings in return.

I spoke to a wonderful mother who was a nurse there. She came during night shifts leaving her two-year-old baby with her husband at home. I could feel the emptiness in her eyes and at the same time, her commitment to work.

I met a 70 year old beautiful woman who looked 55 and she was very proud of it. She told me the secret of this evergreen look - she avoids stress and accepts life however it comes. She forgives and moves on.

I spoke to a young nurse who had just graduated in nursing. She told me her job needed a lot of patience. She learned to be calm - Don't react but respond!

A little girl and I played together without knowing each other. A balloon was enough to make her giggle. She taught me to live in the moment.

Last but not least, I felt proud of my father when he refused to sit in the wheelchair on his last day at the hospital. He said he could manage to walk. I learnt that mental strength is more powerful than physical strength.

Meditate

I am a person who is always restless. I sit, I walk, I work, I drive and even when I sleep, my mind is always working.

I am sure you too face this. You are talking to someone, but your inner chatter is cooking something else at the same time.

There is huge traffic in your mind. One thought goes, another comes and one more is ready to cross the road.

You are so occupied. This leads to a mess because you stop getting new ideas, you are busy only with repetitive thoughts, worries and assumptions.

If it is so, be careful.

The way you clear your home cupboard to adjust new things in it, you need to clear your mind too.

Meditate.

This helps you unload unnecessary thoughts from your mind. You don't have to close your eyes and focus on a dot. This is what I have always found difficult.

So don't do it.

Be a witness to your thoughts. Close your eyes and watch them. Check what is coming to the mind. What next and what next!

After a while, you will feel clear. You will empty your mind. You will have space for new thoughts.

This way, you will outlast everyone. Try it.

The Best Thing I Read

The best paragraph I read in SHRIMAD BHAGWAT GITA:

"Krishna tells Arjuna, "If you are seeking validation from outside you, if you are hoping others will praise what a great warrior you are then you are finished. But if you are working from within, for your inner peace and satisfaction, then do whatever you want. Why do you not want to fight? Because people will say you fought your family? Whatever is meant to happen will happen. There is no certainty that you will win, nor that you will lose. Why are you so tense? Don't expect to be perfect. Nobody is, including me. Don't run after accolades. Just do your karma."

I feel motivated whenever I read this paragraph in our holy book Shrimad Bhagwat Gita. This gives me immense confidence and courage to shun the fear of being judged by others. "What will people say?" doesn't matter to me now. I believe in being myself and acting how I feel relevant for myself and my life.

I neither look for approval from others nor give explanations to them about things that I do. I learnt that I can't please everyone around me. When Krishna, being the lord, couldn't meet everyone's expectations, how can I? I am just an ordinary human being.

A Day at the Bank

I had some work in the bank. It was crowded, so I joined the queue.

A woman next to me was telling someone over the phone how much she lacked money and how difficult it was to survive in Bangalore.

A man was consulting a sales executive for a home loan and trying to pick the best option. The interest rate must be less and feasible. I could feel the excitement through his words.

A couple was arguing on an account that the husband wanted to close but the wife wanted to continue as it was from her hometown and probably they needed to change address with proper address proof. Suddenly, it turned into a heated argument.

While I was in a discussion with the bank manager, a young man interfered asking to change his credit card address with the proof of a rental agreement. The manager rejected his request saying the rental agreement is not acceptable.

Since he was staying in a rented house, he had nothing to show as address proof. His sad face was sufficient to tell how homeless he felt.

Till then, I had known the bank to be a financial institution. But, now I got to know how many stories were confined here.

Excuses vs. Dreams

I was sitting in the loo and typing hastily on my mobile.

When I came out, my head was still down and I was engrossed in typing when a colleague asked if I was lost as I did not notice her.

"Ah! No, I am not lost. Sorry, dear. How are you doing?"

And then, we had some chit-chat.

Many people wonder how I manage time for writing. Because I am a working mom.

"This is my passion," I tell them with a subtle smile.

When my baby was small and I was unable to manage time, sometimes I had to take a nap in the office itself. At that time, a Swiss writer asked me to start writing again.

"Are you going insane? I have no time to do anything extra." I said in utter disbelief.

On this, he said everyone has 24 hours only. Don't give an excuse.

He was right. If you are passionate about something, you will definitely do it.

I look at a housewife and find her blessed as she can manage time for her hobbies. This is my opinion.

A housewife looks at me and thinks I have a nanny to look after my child, so I'm free to focus on my hobbies. This is her opinion.

A slum child compares his life with the children staying in good apartments and dreams what if I had such a good lifestyle, I could do something in life.

These are excuses. Excuses to escape. Excuses to deceive yourself. I would have done this, I could have done that. This 'would have' and 'could have' create so many illusions. They look nice and lovely in novels, in poetry.

I personally believe life should be full of enthusiasm. Full of adventures. What you want to do, do it. Finish it. Achieve it. Don't grouse that you don't have time. Time is not to be stored and utilized later, time is to be managed at every point of life.

You want to work on your fitness, you want to paint, dance, sing or whatsoever, do that. Find a way.

I remember a saying by Harriet Tubman:

"Every great dream begins with a dreamer. Always remember, you have within you the strength, the patience, and the passion to reach for the stars to change the world."

Life is too short, don't let it go with regrets.

Double Standard

Super duper hit movie Dhadkan was being telecasted on TV.

This movie was overrated at its time.

I just came across the scene where the actress (Shilpa Shetty) was trying to elope with her boyfriend and was caught by her father.

Shilpa Shetty won millions of hearts by staying back and keeping her father's pride high. Because the father gives an emotional speech stating the love and respect a daughter can give, a son cannot but how much a daughter can embarrass the parents, that also a son cannot.

This is not just a movie dialogue but the mentality of our society. This double standard irks me to the core.

If a son gets married to his choice, smokes, drinks or goes for polygamy, it doesn't abuse the parents' reputation but the same action of a daughter does.

Every time a woman is targeted as a piece of morality. She is not free to make her own decisions as her freedom may cause a serious impact on the parents' reputation in society.

And with this, I have a question in my mind - Is the society itself reputed?

Here, every hour a woman is raped, and even babies are not safe. They are molested in their own houses and in public places. They are forced to live life like a slave to their fathers, brothers and husbands. The more they are submissive and silent, the more they are accepted.

A woman is forced to be in a burqa in the name of religion, a woman is considered impure during menstruation and a woman is asked to not to interfere in men's decisions.

A society with such restrictions and beliefs can't be ideal and respectful. We undoubtedly live in a bias society.

Doctors and Their Morality

I grew up observing my father's kindness, patience and compassion as a doctor. He listens to his patients, values them and helps them open up.

Being his daughter, I never felt uncomfortable sharing my physical problems with him. From my first menstruation to pregnancy, I could speak to him about everything.

His young female patients consider him a father figure out of respect. He has brought smiles to countless faces who have been deprived of children for many years and diagnosed as incapable to conceive.

People insist on taking medicines from his hands as they have faith that he has a miraculous blessing. When they touch his feet, his eyes get moist.

When I stepped out of my comfort zone and had to visit other doctors in different cities, I realized that the morals and values were deteriorating in today's young doctors.

During my pregnancy, I was consulting a female doctor in Banaras. She was hyper, loud and impatient though she was known as an experienced doctor in the city. Since it was my first pregnancy and I was to deliver my baby in a few weeks, my nerves were on the edge. But she never consoled me, in fact, she often shouted when she found me hesitant to open up during checkups. I can say that I saw a real demon in her.

Once she yelled at me so badly using absurd words that I switched to another doctor.

In the year 2016, I suffered from dengue. The number of clot-forming cells (platelets) in my bloodstream drastically dropped. I had become too weak and was admitted to one of the best hospitals in Bangalore. I had got severe itching in my legs which didn't let me sleep. I cried and screamed out of pain. The lotion prescribed by the doctor was not working at all. They gave me injections to sleep but at times, this too didn't work. When the doctor came to see me, I told him that this pain was unbearable and I would not survive.

"She has a psychological problem. You should consult a psychiatrist for her." He told my husband.

I was shocked. Later, when I explained this incident to my father's friend who is also a doctor, he laughed.

"We often encounter such patients who claim to not survive anymore. This is very common. When the pain gets unbearable, what else one can say? They need treatment from the doctor, not counselling" He said firmly.

Doctors are considered the second form of God. So, we trust them but in today's world, some are simply there to ruin our faith.

The Ideology

How could you be such a fool? I don't believe, you rejected an NRI." A friend exclaimed when we were sharing our life stories during a tea break.

When I was going through arrange marriage process, there was this boy who was settled in the USA. He wanted to marry me as he had seen me years ago at a family get-together. He was nice and decent. I spoke to him over the calls and liked him but still, I couldn't accept the proposal.

I had just started my career at that time and I was doubtful about getting a job in the USA. I didn't want to become a housewife.

When this friend mocked me for rejecting such a well-settled groom, I wondered if a woman's wish is only to settle down with a successful man. Because I am the woman to whom her self-satisfaction and independence matter a lot.

Later, I received many proposals where men insisted that I should be quitting my job and be a homemaker after marriage.

I am not writing this to offend them. It was absolutely their choice of how they wanted to see their wives and I respect that. I am only writing here about what matters to me.

Well, what I had been aspiring for all my life was totally based on my observation. I had seen the women mostly being submissive in their family as they were not earning.

"Follow me" was the tag the men of their family had been carrying for years. And surprisingly, I didn't see any sign of this tag getting weaker as the women too accepted it wholeheartedly.

So there was nothing to accuse a specific gender. However, personally, I could not fix myself with this tag.

The reason behind this was my own ideology towards life. I wanted to be independent - both mentally and financially. I did not like to depend on my father or husband for my daily needs.

Also, I have always been fond of my identity. I did not like to be known as someone's daughter or wife. My self-esteem and aspirations motivated me to get recognition.

I wanted to dress up every morning and leave home like a warrior.

Moreover, I have a different opinion about managing the house and the kids. There are many people who are looking for a job as domestic help. What if I can employ them to look after my house and use my intelligence in something more productive?

This is how I have viewed my life. And I wish this is how every woman could view it, then the miseries in their life would have been lesser.

Things that Keep Me Serene

I had arguments with my neighbours. They had been unnecessarily troubling me.

They are all well-educated, degree holders but senseless people. Looking at their activities, if I call them mentally sick, I won't be wrong.

Every day, they try to find something to hurt me. Initially, I used to feel emotional and taking everything to my heart. I was wondering what sort of people they were. I was losing my mind.

But soon, I got myself back on the track. I made myself understand that they are mud. If I throw a stone in the mud, my clothes will only get dirty. So I trained myself not to pay heed to them.

I taught myself that the world is full of varieties of people. They can't be the same. And also, I can't change them. I can only change myself and my perspective on the world.

I started maintaining a distance from unworthy people. 'Interact less and retain your peace' is my mantra nowadays.

I try to see the abundance around me, like fresh air, rain, sun and the ground under my feet. I thank the universe for everything that I have.

I avoid negative thoughts — negative thoughts about myself and even my surroundings.

I read the book, "Who will cry when you die" written by Robin Sharma. To be honest, this book has helped me a lot to keep myself focused. I recommend my readers read self-help books. These books teach us the art of living.

I always try to feed good thoughts to my mind. I smile a lot while walking in the morning. I visualize how I am leading a beautiful life.

At times, I feel fatigued. I then write journals and vent out my frustration. Sometimes, I connect with good friends or my family members who motivate me.

Silence is another important medium that helps me keep my mental health intact. I embrace the silence - the complete silence. No noise in my head, I just feel blank. I don't talk, don't think about anything. This helps me re-create myself.

The Desire of Being Wanted

My grandfather was a landlord under British rule. He was a very religious person, spent a lot of time and money building temples and hospitals.

I hear interesting stories about him from my parents. They say, all his life he was surrounded by people who had a huge respect for him and called him "Dhani Ji".

He didn't work much but spent. He donated lands and money for good deeds. He even travelled a lot.

I believe he was destined to have everything beautiful around. However, in his 80s, when he lost his leg in an accident and needed the support of a wheelchair, the miseries started.

Though he had been a very disciplined person, in terms of his daily rituals, diet and routine, he gradually started being cranky and ill-tempered.

The reason being, as I had observed was to be confined to one room all the time. Now, he needed someone's support to go out which made him frustrated. Out of frustration, he used to shout at everyone. My mother was his major victim as she was close to him and did all his work.

He felt lonely in his late 80s as all his friends already died. Only one person who was a little younger than him and had served him during his young age was alive. At this time, both became close friends. The grandfather desperately waited for him every evening.

My father was too occupied with his profession and my mother was taking care of the household. Children were busy with their studies. I was his favourite and frequently visited his room before and after my school hours but still couldn't fill his loneliness.

He had somehow developed a belief that people didn't listen to him. He thought he had become useless for them. This insecurity agitated him more.

I read, heard, observed and now I believe that people really become children when they grow old. They seek attention and when they don't get it enough, they become tetchy.

I feel, as a human, the most basic thing that we crave is the feeling of being wanted and cherished. Be it any age, we all want to feel loved and needed by others. The moment this feeling seems to weaken, we start feeling useless among our people. We lose interest in our surroundings which leads to disappointment, sadness and depression.

Let's be a little compassionate and make our loved ones, especially old people in the family, feel that their presence still matters.

Being Myself

Sometimes, I don't feel like talking to people. And at times, I have zero interest in knowing them.

The reason is quite simple.

They follow the same monotonous routine. There is nothing new they do which fascinates me. I find them in a race, perspiring and gasping. Everyone has the same goal — Earn, save and invest for children. If it's enough saved for children, then save for the grandchildren.

Everyone is in a competition here. Comparison has made them a psychopath. They are focused on other's life instead of their own. A two-wheeler owner is satisfied in life until his neighbour does not own a car. The moment the neighbour gets a car, the two-wheeler owner starts losing his peace.

Also, they have double standards in everything. They change their ethics as per their convenience. They speak something and have something else in mind. Double standards as well as double faces.

All this doesn't charm me. I had once written a few lines on this in the form of poetry:

"Being myself –

This is what I do

I remain what I am, how I am

I feel good when you like me

I feel empathetic when I receive your hatred

but I remain the same,

more in my own circle

I am humble, I am harsh too

depending all on the circumstances, situation and outer force.

At times, I am humble, aggressive, revolutionary and indignant.

I am incapable to hide my restlessness, anger and emotions.

Though I don't stand with the flock,

there are people in it

who like me carry myself without the mask

in this super suspicious, dodgy world"

So I prefer to be myself. I invest my energy in things that I love to do. I am not anti-social. I have a few friends — different from the crowd. I spend time with them with the intention to learn something new and grow. I believe they too come to me with the same intention.

Instead of wasting time knowing the same kind of people, I prefer to be with Tagore, Osho, Robin Sharma, Paulo Coelho and many more. These legends keep giving me the confidence to keep my personality intact, whether it is liked by the crowd or not.

I try to be available for myself. I spare time to go for a stroll and have self-talk. Being myself and staying away from unnecessary drama has helped me evolve into a better version of myself.

Freedom

Once one of my readers asked me what was the most beautiful thing in the whole world.

And my answer was freedom.

Freedom to live your life how you want.

I come across many men and women who lose their freedom in the name of love and possessiveness. They simply become each other's property.

"Please stay away, he is mine. Or don't dare to look at her, she belongs to me." No doubt, it feels good when we hear such a statement from our lovers.

But somewhere this causes slavery. You cannot look beyond. You cannot view the other part of the world as you have confined yourself to this one person. And here, your learning stops.

I know a few women who have been intelligent. They could become dancers, musicians, professors, pilots and engineers. But they couldn't do anything and ended up being just a housewife. Because they had no freedom to pursue their dreams.

I know a few old couples living with their son and daughter-in-law. At this last moment of life when they are done with worldly affairs, they wish to live a beautiful life, full of love, romance, care and peace. But they have no freedom to do so. Their grown-up kids would question them as if they are committing a crime.

In our country, still falling in love and getting married to our lover is not appreciable. The young generation is still not free to choose a life partner on their own.

Women are still being judged on having male friends. Men are accused of extramarital affairs if they wish to spend some time with a female friend after marriage.

How can we be so narrow-minded? Do we ever think, many lives are dying every day due to the intolerance that our society shows?

Every happy-looking face is hiding some sadness. We need to see them closely, in order to find reality.

P. S.- I talk about freedom, not freakishness. The difference you need to understand.

Possessiveness

There was some construction work going on near my house. They were building an apartment.

It was Monday morning and I was rushing to the office. Suddenly, I heard a disturbing sound. One worker was beating his woman. When the others came to rescue her, he shouted at them and said that she was his wife. He could do whatsoever he wanted to do with her.

He had a point. She was his wife, his property.

So people who had gathered with full of enthusiasm, slowly dispersed.

I agree with Osho who says the idea of marriage and family is destructive. These institutions encourage possessiveness.

"This is my child. I can do whatever I want to do with him" - have you heard parents stating such nonsense?

Your child, your man or your woman are individuals, cannot be your property. They are not your chair, house or car that you can possess. Possessiveness is poison. It is destructive. It is violent.

It destroys freedom. It doesn't let you move freely. Due to dependencies, you are always bound to be obedient. Your child has to be obedient for his survival, or else you will thrash him. This is so scary.

You married your man or woman, he/she became your property. You say, "don't look at him/her, he/she is mine." - This is so absurd.

A man, a woman or a child is not a thing that you can monopolize. But the institution called family encourages such behaviour.

If you carefully notice, a man starts learning corruption, politics, and hatred from the very beginning, in the family itself. Not all families, but 99% belong to this category only. A child starts losing his innocence. Convince your parents, children, spouse and get things done. Bribe them and get things done. You call it skill-learning and I call it corruption.

Such families are rarely found which are based on love, where people gather to share happiness. In most families, one or the other is suffering, one or the other is playing dirty politics.

But still, we sing the song, "we are united, we are united."

I find this absolutely ridiculous.

Small Things Matter

A few years ago, a friend got married. I met her recently and found that she was no more that happy go lucky girl. I could read her sad face.

When I asked her the reason behind that sadness, her answer left me thinking, *"Yes, small things matter."*

She told me that her husband was a good person but he never appreciated her. He never complimented her for her cooking, appearance or anything. She felt more offended when she was criticized by him.

I asked if he did not love her.

She told me that he loved her, but never expressed it. She confessed that he criticized her for her faults, not just like that. But the reason why she felt violent at that time was she never got an appreciation for her good things.

So criticism gave her an inferiority complex. She craved for beautiful words from her husband, which could compensate for the bitterness at the time of criticism.

We often take relationships for granted.

"Oh! She is a mother; her job is to take care of children. She is a wife; taking care of household chores is her responsibility."

My colleague's wife was an excellent cook. We enjoyed the food that she packed for her husband. Many times, I asked him if he conveyed our appreciation. He said that he did **sometimes**.

I asked why not every day, as we admired daily? He told me that this was her job. According to him, appreciating every day loses its value.

I was shocked. To be honest, I did not like it. Doesn't she deserve lovely words for her great work? Preparing delicious food every day does not lose its value, but appreciating every day does. Isn't it strange?

I believe, we have a wrong mindset.

Appreciation is an encouragement. It heals sick people, excels the talent. It helps relationships get better.

Mental Independence

When I revealed my marital status as divorced in a blog on social media and wrote how I walked out of a toxic marriage, many women tried seeking my advice.

A young woman named Rachna approached me with a strange story:

She is working in a multinational company in Mumbai. Before marriage, she had been on business trips to many foreign countries. She was independent and strong.

However, after the marriage, things changed. Her husband underestimates her and often makes her feel worthless.

She earns a handsome salary but she has no control over her account. She is totally dependent on her husband for every single penny. Until her husband doesn't allow her, she can't spend.

According to her husband and mother in law, she can travel to her mother's place only with a male from her family. Since her father is no more and her brother is too young to travel, she is unable to visit her mother's place. She herself wonders thinking if she could travel to far countries all alone, why can't she go to her hometown alone?

She tells me how she is criticized by her husband and mother in law for every work she does at home. They are always keen to prove her wrong. She is blamed, demeaned and tortured.

After being with them for the last two years, finally, she has lost her confidence. She feels depressed and suicidal.

She cannot go for divorce as she doesn't have courage. She is afraid of her relatives and neighbours in her hometown. How will they react after knowing her marital status if she goes for divorce?

Earlier I thought that financial independence is everything in a woman's life. But after knowing Rachna's story I realised that being mentally independent is more important than being financially independent. There are many Rachnas in our country who are well educated and settled in their career but their confidence level is zero. They are unaware of their potential. And this causes huge miseries in their life.

Why is it so?

Because Indian parents fail to give their daughters the greatest lesson of life - Having the courage to fight against all the odds. Education and career are still not enough to make a woman independent, she must be taught to have a clear vision for her life, future, needs and wants.

I was myself living in a dilemma. I knew I was not happy in my marriage but I had no guts to come out of it.

I was scared of living alone. I had no confidence to lead a life, taking all the responsibilities of a child on my own. On top of that, I was warned that I would be a broke if I break the marriage. So every time I thought of dissolving the marriage, my heart thumped with fright. However, the constant pain of the toxic relationship was not letting me live either. I had developed a thin border between living in a loveless marriage and living life on my own. The border had to be broken and to do so, it needed a huge amount of courage that I didn't have.

With time, I realised I would die on this side as well as that side. Then why not take a risk and see what is there, on the other side of the borderline.

This curiosity gave me the courage to break the line. And after breaking it, life got easier, at least it met my expectations.

I wish Rachna too had learnt to take risks and be ready to face its consequences, be it positive or negative. Decision-making is important for our survival and I personally feel, each of us must learn it, irrespective of gender.

Sooner or Later

I saw tears in his eyes.

He was my manager in my last company. An introvert who was brilliant but reticent. He always spoke less in meetings. No bragging, no making noise.

He had joined the company as an intern but soon earned enough name and fame due to his outstanding performance. After a few years, he was promoted to the post of the manager.

He was a very kind person and in a short time, we became lunch partners. Though we used to have fun, I had a huge respect for him.

After working in the same domain for many years, He wanted to explore a new profile, hence he applied for another department. He was shortlisted and happily joined there.

Still, we used to have our lunch together. After a few weeks, he started feeling uncomfortable. He found a lot of politics there. He tried hard to mingle with people, but no one was ready to accept him.

People were not ready to give him the know-how and expected him to finish work on time.

He kept his points in front of management, but no result.

He felt low and dejected.

And suddenly, one day he got a mail about being fired.

I couldn't meet his eye when he told me about his home loan and wife's pregnancy.

He left the job.

But sometimes, a few things happen for the good. After 2–3 months, he was placed in a reputed MNC with a better position and package. The company keeps sending him abroad.

I see that happy face on Facebook. It really feels good.

My mom is right. She says, sooner or later, good people always receive good things.

Sex

Once, a friend told me a very strange thing. She said if I watch sex videos on YouTube, I won't be able to control my sexual urges. I will start looking for a partner.

"Is it? Let me try it." I thought to myself.

So one fine day, I watched a few videos for a few hours. It didn't affect me.

I watched it again regularly for 2-3 days, just believing in my friend's statement. I waited for an outcome.

And then finally, I had an outcome. I found these videos utterly mad and neurotic. I banged my head looking at them. I didn't find any productivity in their action, except reproducing a child. And the child too will be neurotic as it came out of neurotic actions.

I found them trapped by worldly affairs. The way they presented sex shows their gluttony.

And therefore, it didn't impress me, and nor did I fall for it. I felt I have better work to do than this. The pleasure I get from my writing is more than any sort of feeling. I find productivity here as many people message me stating how my words are changing their life.

Well, I am not against sex. I am not a saint. However, my belief about sex is different from others.

I believe sex is divine. It's a pause where two people become one. They start worshipping each other, instead of just satisfying their urges. At that moment, feelings for each other get so intense that tears roll down. One bends down to touch/ kiss the partner's feet. Sex is an act to express/feel the depth of love.

How many people experience this? I think no one in today's world. Sex is just a need for them. It is just a part of the daily routine. Some of them use it as a weapon to convince their partner or coax them to do things in their favour. One doesn't like one's spouse. They keep squabbling throughout the day but at night they have sex. Do you think sex can be divine for them?

I feel blessed that I am no more in that race.

Karma Strikes Back

Raghav uncle and Suhana aunty had been leading a peaceful life. They had only one son. Uncle was running a small shop and Aunty used to stitch clothes for livelihood. They did not have much, but they were satisfied with whatever they had.

Their goal was to bring up the son, though they had limited resources.

When the son grew up, he started his business. He was doing great in business. He got married. His wife appeared to be very selfish. She did not want to stay with her in-laws, she even provoked the husband against the parents. They got separated from their parents and built a new room and kitchen on top of the house. They had two children. But nobody paid attention to the old parents.

The old couple was sad. They had never thought they would be mistreated by their son.

Once Raghav uncle fell sick and could not resume his shop again. The shop was closed forever. Suhana aunty was still stitching the clothes for livelihood.

I once visited them. Looking at their situation, tears rolled down my cheeks. Suhana aunty told me how her daughter-in-law taunts her with arrogance.

"A woman whose husband doesn't work has to stitch the clothes only. I can't do such a job." The daughter-in-law had said.

Hearing this, I felt shocked.

"How could one be so harsh to their own people?" I had no answer to this question.

That day I left their home with a heavy heart.

After a few years, I heard again about them. This time, the news was different. The son had lost his business and was in huge debt. People visited the home searching for him. He got tired of convincing them. In stress, he fell sick. His legs got swollen and he was unable to walk. He was depressed and his blood pressure was falling.

I was again shocked. This time I was shocked at nature's response. Karma strikes back!

Suhana aunty is still stitching the clothes......

Teaching is an Art

In one of my jobs, I had a senior colleague about whom everyone said she had a superiority complex.

When I joined the organization, we were a batch of 26 people and she was our trainer.

She had joined the organization just a year ago but she quickly got a hold of the work procedure. She was intelligent and a good speaker as well.

I even observed the seniors clarifying their doubts with her. Our managers too liked her a lot.

She was good at heart but she used to lose patience while explaining things. Sometimes she shouted at people.

Due to this behaviour, people didn't feel comfortable with her and often criticized her. They had expected politeness from her but she failed to meet their expectation.

I felt she had no bad intentions. Still, she was not liked by many. And I wished she could work on it.

When we work in a team, our behaviour matters a lot. Maybe you are more ingenious than others but you need to maintain some courtesy. The majority of people are average-minded. You need to be calm, patient and polite with them.

I remember an incident. I was a fresher and was new to corporate culture. I joined an MNC just after completing my studies.

There was a team meeting and the team lead, who was a trainer too, was explaining something. I didn't understand something in that, hence I asked a cross-question. She made fun of me stating someone should explain to me in Hindi as my mother tongue is Hindi. The whole team laughed at this lame joke. I felt embarrassed. Being an introverted and emotional person, it hurt me a lot and that day, I came home in tears.

In recent years, I have been teaching German to corporate people with whom I have experienced the best thing. My students were were young men and women. Still, they took a lot of time to grasp the language. With them, I understood that learning depends on our interests. How much are we interested to learn something or are we learning it just because we need it in our profession?

I understood that everyone can't be a quick learner. As a teacher and a trainer, I need to have patience while making them grasp the basics. I remember how my uncle used to teach the students. He was a doctor and a visiting faculty in the high school where I had studied. He taught Sanskrit to students. While explaining a story in Sanskrit or teaching grammar, he drew pictures on the blackboard, just to bring interest among students. The students had fun learning Sanskrit grammar.

A teacher or trainer is a person who can do miracles for his students. No doubt, teaching is an art!

Unbelievable

My friend Maya has always been close to me. She hails from Punjab. We joined an organisation together and found a great companionship in each other.

We spent a lot of time together. With time, we started sharing our personal lives with each other.

When she gained my trust, she shared a strange thing with me. She told me that she married a guy whose mother didn't like her. It was a love marriage and she was madly in love with her husband. The husband too was emotional for her.

This strong bonding was not liked by her mother-in-law. She was a possessive mother and didn't want to share her son with another woman. She did not like their togetherness. When Maya conceived, the mother-in-law started body-shaming her in front of the son. She kept on provoking the son against Maya whenever she was not at home.

Hearing this, I was shocked.

"How could a mother tend to spoil his son's married life?" I asked Maya in disbelief.

At that time, I was not married and was also totally unaware of worldly affairs.

"This is very common in India, Anshu. There is nothing to be surprised about. However, what my mother-in-law did, was not common." She retorted.

She further told me that her mother-in-law regularly met a sorcerer who was very powerful and misused his tantra vidya.

When provoking didn't work to break the relationship, Maya's mother-in-law visited the sorcerer. He gave her a pendant and asked her to put it in a black thread. The pendant should be worn by the son around his neck.

That pendant costed five thousand rupees for which the mother-in-law pestered the son to pay. She convinced him that the pendant would bring abundance and good fortune to his life. He would grow in his career.

Maya was surprised thinking why the pendant costed five thousand rupees. The base of the pendant was neither gold nor silver. The stone in it was just an ordinary stone.

However, she could not oppose it as her husband got convinced by his mother.

After wearing this pendant, her husband started behaving strangely. He unnecessarily got angry at Maya for every small thing. He shouted at her for no reason. They started fighting. Maya lost her mental peace. She was getting depressed and at times, she cried nonstop. But her tears couldn't melt her husband.

This went on for a month. One afternoon, the fight got so severe that Maya tried to commit suicide by taking sleeping pills. Looking at this, her husband got furious and slapped her. She held his collar in anger and in this mayhem, she suddenly pulled his pendant. It broke and fell down on the floor.

As soon as it got separated from his body, he calmed down, hugged her and wept. He implored her to not take this harsh step stating how he would live without her.

After that, they both realised that the pendant was evil. They threw it right away. Since then, her husband stopped listening to his mother. Maya's life got better.

Later, she told me that she shared this story with a colleague Radhika from Manipur who confirmed that tantra Vidya or black magic exists. And even, she had herself been the victim of it. Now, this is another story.

Radhika had a boyfriend whom she wanted to marry. But her parents didn't like him as he was from a different caste. They started persuading her to change her mind. But Radhika was not ready and continued her relationship with her boyfriend in Bangalore.

Once she visited her hometown in Manipur. Her parents gave her a ring to wear saying this would protect her from evil eyes. She wore it. After coming to Bangalore, she started fighting with her boyfriend. For no reason, she threatened him to break this relationship. She was herself disturbed and one day, somehow she removed the ring. After removing it, her mental status became stable. She felt lighter in her mind. She was full of regrets and desperately wanted her boyfriend back. Now, they are happily married.

Later, when Radhika confronted her mother, she confessed that the ring came after consulting a sorcerer as she was not happy with this relationship.

For me, both stories were unbelievable. We live in an era, where we believe in science. But there are a few things beyond science that science couldn't clarify. There is some power - both good and bad, probably they are the only god and devils. And this prevails across the country.

We are Indians

My colleague Rajan is a little sophisticated. He considers himself modern and insists on making changes without paying heed to one's sentiments.

Once, during a lunch break at the office, he told me about an event where he went out for dinner with his German teammates. In the restaurant, a person was eating by hand. Seeing that, the German colleague asked him if it is common in India.

"I am from north India and in the north, we don't eat with hands, we use spoons. But in the southern part of India, people do." Rajan answered.

While telling this to me, I could feel the sense of pride in his voice. However, to me, he sounded like a divider between north and south India. It seemed that he had not learnt to respect different cultures.

Before I could speak anything, he started exaggerating about his family and how everyone at his home eats with spoons. He expressed his disgust for people who eat with their hands.

I don't know how the German colleagues reacted, but I am sure that it must have surprised them. As far as I know Germans, they are always proud of their country, culture and language.

'We are Indians beyond this south and north." Rajan could not keep it simple in front of the guests.

I could not speak much or I would say, I preferred to be quiet. However, I kept on thinking about how much hatred or aversion we carry for each other in our own country. We are grown up. We consider ourselves well qualified, and sophisticated but we don't know how to respect our people, their cultures and lifestyles.

India is a country where unity lies in diversity. We need to understand this. We need to respect others and their behaviours/cultures. Our maturity is nothing if we cannot accept the diversification. We need to think twice before we react. Our statement might hurt someone. Life is not all about status, standard or style. If we focus on humanity, life would be meaningful.

Imperfection vs Opportunity

The Geography teacher in my high school was a wise man. I grew fond of his personality and perspective of looking at things from a different angle. I was his favourite student though I always argued with him on topics that he threw in the class with a different perspective.

Once he shared his opinion about America. He said he didn't like America as a developed country. He liked Asian and African countries including India which are still developing or under development.

"How can you say that? Don't you see how much poverty and unemployment we have? We don't even have good infrastructure for health and education." I pointed out in utter astonishment, being an economics student.

He smiled which confused me more. He said he would explain to me after the class.

After the class, he took me out to the school garden and showed me a hibiscus plant. I didn't understand what he was going to explain.

"Look at this red flower and other buds. The flower is completely bloomed. And the buds are yet to bloom. Which one do you find beautiful?" He asked.

"Of course, the flower." I quickly answered.

"But I find the buds more beautiful. The flower is now going to dry and fall. It is going to lose its beauty and charm but the buds have the opportunity to grow. They are yet to work on their imperfections." He explained further.

"You are right. But I still did not understand how could you connect this to developing and developed countries?" I asked.

"Look, America is developed now. Americans don't have to do anything for their growth. They are at their peak and now you know what happens after reaching the peak, don't you?" He smiled again.

Later, he told me that Americans might use their resources in future to destroy things as they don't have to do anything productive in their own country. They might create unnecessary wars and become the reason for destruction whereas the developing countries would still be occupied with creating/inventing new things to make life easier and more beautiful.

In later years, I realised how right my teacher was. I learnt about the Wabi-sabi concept which came from Japan. This concept shows us the beauty of the imperfect nature of the world around us. Imperfections give us a chance to grow. It teaches us to appreciate the beauty of imperfection as an opportunity for growth.

A Letter to My Son

Dear Evaan,

I still remember those nine months, carrying you in my womb. The suffering was intense and my pregnancy symptoms were not normal. I had to go through rejection by many doctors.

Your grandparents (My parents) supported me through thick and thin. When I was losing my patience, they assured me that this phase would pass soon. I believed them. They too suffered with me and, went to many temples for blessings. Blessings for you, blessings for me!

The D day arrived, and again I suffered like hell. The doctors declared that they would be able to save only one - either you or me. Your grandparents could not take it. I had been their loveliest child, how could they afford to lose me? And you? You were going to be their youngest grandchild.

Being himself a doctor, your grandfather folded his hands, with tears in his eyes and begged the doctor to save both of us. Your grandmother kept on chanting Mahamrityunjay Mantra until you came to this earth.

However, unaware of all that was happening outside, I was screaming out of pain in the operation theatre, perspiring and gasping. And finally, after hours of struggle, the teams of doctors succeeded. We both survived.

When I saw you for the first time, I forgot all my suffering.

"*You delivered a boy*", this is what the nurse had told me enthusiastically throwing you on my bosom. And I felt a surge of being more responsible. I wanted to be a mother who nurtures a man wisely.

I want you to become a real man who believes in humanity. A man who respects women. A person who cannot hurt anyone.

I want to teach you - As you sow so you reap. I want you to know that life is all about a "give and take policy". So before hurting anyone, think twice.

Before wishing ill for anyone, think of the almighty.

There is a power that runs the whole universe. It is everywhere, watching you. It knows to love us and punish too. So fear it.

Be a good, supporting and caring husband. The day you decide to marry, keep your ego aside first. Being your mother, I would always expect a smile on your girl's face which would appear because of you.

Last but not least, I would keep a stock of everything that I have done for you. Not to show as a favour but as a reminder to you, that you too get your turn to look after me, once I become a child again. I expect you to not get annoyed, when I ask you the same question repeatedly, *"Who is there at door?"*.

Because I have answered your questions a thousand times when you were small.

I expect you to hold my hand and take me to the washroom when my body becomes frail and emaciated. I want you to sit with me every day, and talk. Ask me if I am alright if I need something.

If you are too busy in your life, you can drop me at Old Age Home. I won't mind. At least, this would be better than you losing your patience and misbehaving with me.

My child! I just want you to be a good human being.

How I Started Working on Myself?

There have been many factors.

When people, whom I had loved with my heart and soul, rejected me, I felt like working on myself instead of feeling depressed and forlorn.

It's not like I didn't feel depressed but I wanted to prove myself to them. The rejection gave me the fuel to be resilient.

I take things on my ego. However, I don't let this ego misguide me and then indulge in bitter feelings. I just forgive them and focus on myself with a belief that one day they might regret to the wrong they have done to me.

I have been a Hindi medium student until class 10th. My college was a convent where I took some time to adjust to the English medium though I was known as a bright student. Most of the students in the college were from English medium and knew my background. At times, their fluency in English unnerved me. But now, the same students ask me how I speak and write so well in English.

Would you believe English has become my mother tongue now? I am more comfortable speaking and writing in English than in my mother tongue which is Hindi.

How? I worked on myself with a zeal to achieve what others had.

I am blessed to have a beautiful family and some friends who motivated me during my bad time.

I read good books. They have always been my guide. I got strength from them to rebuild my life.

All my student life, I wrote journals. I shared my feelings, vulnerability and desires with my diary. Every day I told my diary that I wouldn't give up. This helped me evolve into a person who is adamant about her beliefs, flexible to change her belief if required and strong enough to not surrender to the circumstances.

I have become Antifragile.

Live in the Present Moment

Last month I got to know that all the parents would be sending their kids to offline school this year. They had started taking admission.

I was late as I had thought I would continue with the same online school this year as well where my child is currently studying. I am really afraid of Covid.

When I consulted a friend for her opinion on this, she straightforwardly advised me to send him to an offline school. She was already sending her kids to school.

Now, I got anxious as I had to find a good school and take admission for my child. My friend had advised me to visit a few schools and look at their infrastructure closely. That would help me find a better school.

Summer had arrived. And it was quite hot outside. However, I immediately visited three schools within 6 kilometres, but couldn't choose any.

Called many people (known and unknown) to get their feedback about these schools and others as well.

One or another thing was disappointing me in every school. I felt helpless. Exhausted too.

I wished for my ex-husband.

"If he was there, at least he had taken the responsibility for our child. I wouldn't have to face everything alone."

I regretted my divorce. When I shared this feeling with a friend, he told me a very wise thing.

"We humans often tend to forget our miseries and underestimate the pain that we had gone through in the past," he said.

How true it is!

After a few days, when things were settled, I thought about my regrets again. And then, I realised that we humans don't live in the moment. We worry about the past and future which is totally irrelevant. Out of control.

Buddhism and even stoicism say that the present is all that exists. The past is gone, our regrets won't change it. And the future is unseen.

The Stoics insist on the impermanence of things around us. Our sorrow, our happiness — everything is fleeting.

I was getting worried about the future - "If I am struggling so much to decide on a school, how will I manage his higher education alone?"

If I can worry about the unseen future, why can't I focus on thinking positive and hoping for the best? Who knows if I will have a bunch of brilliant people in future who will guide me in my child's education?

Many people consider me courageous. I believe the inception of this courage is living in the moment which I always try to do.

Would you now live in the moment?

Living in Unknown Fear

"Will see what happens."

This is what I carelessly say to myself when I am distraught.

The past is gone. My regret and remorse can't change it. What happened, happened. By regretting I can only gain hypertension which will spoil my future too.

Worrying about the future is also not going to help. If I am destined to lose something, I will. Likewise, if I am destined to gain something, I will. I leave a few things to the universe and let it decide for me.

I cry when I feel like doing so. And I laugh when I want to.

I prefer to live in the moment. And I love this present moment to bits and pieces. I embrace things that I have, without worrying about losing them in future. I don't get into relationships with my family and friends with the hope that they will assist me during my tough time.

I don't care if my neighbours are cordial with me or not. I am not afraid of this thought, 'who will help me at midnight if

anything happens to me or my baby as I am a single mother'.
I don't live in fear.

If I believe in God, then why fear? He will send someone
to help me when I need it. And if he wants me to suffer
more, I will accept that too. However, why think negative?
If I have not done wrong to anyone, nothing drastic would
happen to me.

Have faith. And I do have it.

So, live in the moment. Learn that you cannot change your
destiny no matter how powerful you are. Yes, you can make
constant efforts to improve your life. You can strengthen your
mental state to accept the circumstances and live happily
forever. And yes, don't forget to find happiness in every little
thing the way I do.

I have come across many people who live in baseless
fear and insecurities and ruin their present. My aunt is a great
example of it.

She was a lovely woman. She had a son who was well
settled in his business. In fact, the business was growing day
by day.

However, the aunt always lived in fear. What if the son
encounters failure in business? The market is so competitive.

Whenever I met her and we talked about her son's
successful business, she displayed her assumptions.

"He is careless. He doesn't eat food on time. He might have
gastric problem. He doesn't listen to me. He has to keep an

eye on his competitors but he takes things easy." I could hear such overwhelming concerns from her.

I know she is a mother and a mother is always worried about her children. However, the way my aunt was assuming things and was getting worried, clearly showed that she was living in fear.

She was afraid of unseen events which were causing anxiety to her. She was not able to think positive because of her fear. It was not only impacting her health but also her mental state was getting affected.

At some point in time, I too lived in fear.

"How would I manage everything alone as a single mother? What would happen if my child faced any difficulties? Whom would I call if there was an emergency? What if I lose my job again?" Such thoughts frightened me to my bones.

And then, anxiety became my companion. I slept with anxiety and woke up with anxiety as if life and anxiety were going parallel.

After a lot of practice, when I overcame my fear and trusted the universe to be kind to me, not only did my anxiety reduce but also I became audacious.

So if you want to overcome your anxiety, you have to first overcome your fear.

I Love You

My six year old son wrote 'I Love you' to my friend's four year old daughter and handed over the chit to her.

This incident took place 2 to 3 times which I was totally unaware of. But I knew my son considered the girl his best friend and absolutely adored her.

However, after this incident, I got a call from my friend who was furious at this and shouted at me. She didn't like this deportment of my child.

I apologised to her over the call but couldn't take her anger. I lost my temper and beat my son while crying myself. I think this is a typical trait of all mothers.

After a few days, when I recalled the incident with peace of mind, I realised how badass my son was. I felt proud of him as well as my upbringing. I felt proud of being a mother of such an expressive boy. At this tender age, he is capable of finding ways to express himself.

It didn't take much time for me to understand how he learnt this behaviour. My ex-husband never expressed his feelings to me which I had always craved for. So gradually, I developed a belief that we must learn to express our feelings to our loved ones. This helps to strengthen the relationship and build trust.

So I decided to instill this habit in my son. I made sure my son and I often say I love you to each other, with a reason and also, without any reason. Every night we exchange goodnight kisses before we sleep. We let each other know how grateful we are to have each other in our life.

But here, I had made a mistake. I couldn't teach my son that the society, we live in, has its own norms and rules. Here one can slap another in public but saying 'I love you' would be a big 'No-No'. Here one can murder someone in broad daylight but a couple kissing each other can't be accepted. In fact, it's a crime!

I had thought I would establish a beautiful world for my son where love could be expressed and harmony could be easily found. What a simpleton I was!

Suffering With no Solution

Shobhna Aunty is no more.

My mother tells me that she led a miserable life at the age of 60. Her husband suspected her of having an extramarital affair.

The woman who had always been chirpy and positive towards life suddenly became quiet. She kept on proving herself right and explaining to her husband that she was not involved in such an ugly act, but the husband didn't believe her.

He locked her in a room whenever he had to go out. At night, he kept the keys under his pillow after locking the house as if Shobhna aunty will elope with his imaginary boyfriend.

The husband was suffering from depression and had become a psychopath.

Shobhna Aunty initially endured all the harassment thinking that Goddess Sita too had to prove herself righteous in Ramayana. She was just a human and this might be a phase of life. However, deep down, she was feeling broken. She was condemned to have done something that she couldn't even imagine in her dreams.

She was unable to share this hideous blame with anyone. For her, the respect of her husband and family was extreme and it must remain intact.

So she let the husband create an unnecessary fuss day and night. According to her, it was better as it was inside the four walls only. She suffered and shed tears alone and gradually lost her life inside those four walls only.

In today's world where we claim to be advanced and modern, a woman irrespective of her age suffers everywhere - Sometimes in the family and sometimes outside. In India, psychological issues are still underestimated and visiting a psychiatrist is a big deal. Consulting a marriage counsellor is not encouraged here. That's why there are countless failed marriages. Though there are not many divorce cases as it is not in our culture, the couples feel suffocated and crestfallen.

I wish the psychological issues and visiting a psychiatrist/ marriage counsellor could be normalised the way it is in western countries.

Lack of Empathy

I remember an incident from childhood.

I was 13-14-year-old, attending a small function at my relative's house. I was a quiet girl. I did not speak much if I was not comfortable with people. So I was just observing things around.

A cousin who was married and was twice my age started bashing me. According to her, I looked rustic. I had no sense of fashion. She had always stayed in big cities and was proud of it. She asked me if I did not get any other dress to wear as the one I was wearing was so weird.

I had tears in my eyes which I tried hard to hide from her. I succeeded too but soon had to rush to the washroom to let them flow freely.

I lost my confidence for that day. Throughout the function, I kept quiet and was unable to have eye contact with anyone considering myself rustic.

In our family, she is known to be as outspoken. But I hated her for this same quality. I still remember her for the same incident and never have good feelings for her.

I wish everyone had a little compassion. A little empathy everyone could hold in themselves, the world would be a much better place. But it seems the world is falling short of empathy nowadays.

P.S. — The same lady now admires me for being independent and looking good and fit. However, it doesn't impress me.

Spirituality

In the journey of my life, I came across many men and women with whom I got a chance to exchange views. Some were genuine and interacting with them, I learnt different aspects of life which I was not aware of. However, some of them wore totally fake personalities. With them, I realised that there are many people in this world who carry double standards. Either they say something and do something else or they appear absolutely different than they are in reality.

I met a man who was always keen to talk to me. I knew him as a respectful person in the society. So initially, I responded to him well. But soon, I started getting fed up. The more I avoided him, the more I was caught up. If he once began to talk, it didn't seem that he would take a break and let me go. While waiting for the elevator or in the basement, I often encountered him.

He got to know that reading was my area of interest and I admire Osho. So he started talking about spirituality and exaggerating how spiritual he was.

One day he told me a very strange thing. He said he has abandoned the luxuries of life. He has even left his wife and child as he got into spirituality.

"Is he another Gautama?" I was amazed.

Later he told me that he doesn't kill the cockroaches, rats and mosquitoes in his house because spirituality doesn't allow him to do so.

I was taken aback.

Since we were living in the same apartment, I knew we had enough rats and cockroaches here. In fact, we had mosquitoes too which cause 'Dengue'. In the year 2016, I had suffered from dengue and was admitted to the hospital. I almost felt like I fought between life and death. Since then I have become extra careful. If I see a sign of a mosquito at home, I immediately turn on the ultra power 'all out'.

And this man was saying that he let the mosquitoes, rats and cockroaches enter the home as he follows spirituality. He emphasized that killing anything is against humanity.

I wanted to ask him a simple question and I did dare to ask.

"Sir, I appreciate your wisdom and your kindness too. However, I have a question in my mind. What if you get bacteria in your stomach which causes harm to your intestine and you suffer from severe stomachache, wouldn't you visit a doctor? Because the first thing the doctor will do is to give you the antibiotics to kill the bacteria in your stomach." I asked.

He stared at me for a while, stammered a few words which I didn't understand and then suddenly, he realised that he was late and had to rush to the office.

He left. And never came back to me again.

An Evening Without Words

A Bachelor stayed next to our flat. With time, we became good friends.

He was from Tamilnadu. His mom was a kind lady who used to come and stay with him sometimes. I developed a good relationship with her as well.

However, we had a language barrier. I didn't know Tamil and she didn't know Hindi or English. The friend often worked as an interpreter between us. We exchanged our food and at times, the three of us had our coffee together in the evening after I was back from the office.

At that time, I was newly married.

One evening after a fight with my husband, I wanted to impress him by wearing a saree. Since I didn't know how to drape the saree, I knocked on Aunty's door for help.

Unfortunately, the friend was not there for interpretation. I told her I needed her help to wear the saree and she thought I was asking her for a saree. Her face lit up.

She looked overwhelmed.

She quickly opened her cupboard and started showing me many sarees. She was telling me I could take whichever I liked.

And I was telling her I already have a saree, I just needed her help to wear it. She was not understanding me and insisted on the same.

Though I was getting late as my husband was about to come from the office, I felt overwhelmed with this kindness. My eyes got moist.

Somehow I managed to make her understand what I wanted.

And she happily, blissfully helped me wear one.

I still recall that incident fondly. There are people who are amazingly kind and loving. They come forward to offer their affection even to strangers as if the only purpose of their existence is to spread love.

Also, that day I realized love doesn't need to be expressed only through words. There are several ways to demonstrate it.

Raise Your Voice

I was fired....

In one of my corporate jobs, I was fired. The director of the company fired me for no reason.

I was good at work. I had worked on several projects in that organization and established a good rapport with all the managers. But this director mistreated me and I raised my voice. This is when I was fired. There was nothing new in it as there were many employees including HR professionals who got mistreated by him prior to me and ended up losing their jobs.

For this termination, he blamed my performance and told me that I was irregular at work. I had all the proofs in emails that were enough to prove his allegations false. At the beginning of the same year, I had got a 30% hike in my salary because of my performance. Hence, I took this harsh step - I filed a case and pulled him to the police station.

I spoke to a few employees who had faced this termination before me. I requested them to come forward and join me so that we could have enough evidence against the director.

Finally, a woman got ready to support me. Her case was more painful. She had to work for eight months without pay just to get her experience letter. She was furious and resentful of the director's unfair treatment.

I was elated as my case was going to be stronger. There was more hope to get justice now. I asked her to keep all the documents and emails ready. She agreed. But the day she had to arrive at the police station, she withdrew from the commitment.

I felt blue and crestfallen. However, I could not keep quiet as I didn't want more Anshus to suffer. For more than a month, I regularly visited the police station. Sometimes a friend accompanied me and the other times I was alone. There had been times when I sat alone there until 10 PM at night and reached home at 11 PM on my bike, just because the director gave excuses of being busy and appeared too late.

It was an emotional trauma as I felt scared too at times. However, I was not ready to give up. In fact, I did not want to let him go so easily.

To my surprise, he always spoke to the police inspector in the local language Kannada which I did not understand. I wondered how come the director of the company was speaking Kannada whom I had always heard speak English in the office. But he was playing the trick to become friendly with the policemen as they too were Kannada speaking. I had to insist on keeping the communication in English every now and then as I did not understand what he was saying in his defence.

When things did not seem to settle down and I was in despair, I decided to meet a legal advisor. I informed the same to the director in front of the police. And somehow, the police inspector succeeded in doing the settlement between us. Of course, by threatening and scolding the director.

"Look at your age. You are old. How can you mistreat a woman like this? If she goes to court, you will waste both, money and time." The inspector said to him during one of our visits.

And finally, I won the case. I got my experience letter and the salary which he was holding and denied to pay.

After that, everything changed in that organization. The upper management in Germany to which I had sent a mail, took an action. A new policy came where he was no more a dictator. Employees were given their bonuses, even those who had left the organization a few months ago.

There was joy across the company. I got several heartfelt 'Thank you' messages for raising my voice and bringing justice to the organization.

By sharing my story, I would like to encourage you to take a stand whenever needed. Don't keep quiet and move on, learn to raise your voice against injustice. You might not win, but you will get the satisfaction that you didn't tolerate the nonsense. Don't let the world bog you down. Be strong, be genuine, be yourself!

The Marriage Alliance

I am a person who believes in gender equality. I believe, I equally deserve respect and other things that our men deserve. I am the youngest child of my parents who have given me all kind of freedom without differentiating between me and my brother.

So, I could study further, I got myself a job in a Swiss company, and started my life. I was determined that I would marry a man of my choice, but unfortunately, I couldn't find anyone of my type.

Then, there was another way of getting married - arranged marriage! I myself went through the matrimonial sites, called the boys or their family members and fixed the dates for the meeting. Because I didn't want to give any stress on my father. We know very well how arrogant some of the groom's families act in India.

So here, I met some men with whom I went haywire, and lost my temper every time:

I met a man from West Bengal, who was an engineer and liked me in the first meeting itself. But he had a condition that I should quit my job and stay at home. I found it very strange.

I understand I am a woman, and there would be a time when my family might need me. In that case, I am ready to quit. But I cannot do it for life long sacrificing all my desires, degrees, and hard work done for my studies.

He asked if he had to return to his hometown to do business, could I leave everything in Bangalore, and join him there?

"If I get an opportunity to work in Germany for two years, can you join me?" I asked him back.

Him - What if I don't get a job there?

Me: You can stay as a househusband for two years.

Him: How can I?

Me: Then, how can I?

My big "No" to him, and I left.

Then, I met a man from Banaras, who was a scientist. I assumed he must be more understanding than the previous one. But unfortunately, he too failed me. I could smell the patriarchy that was instilled into his personality. He was a vegetarian and asked me if I was a non-vegetarian. I said I love chicken.

"In my family, no one eats non-veg, so I won't allow you to eat chicken after marriage." He said.

The word 'allow' blew me up.

'I was going to be his wife, not his slave, whom he could instruct dos and don'ts.'

However, I left without uttering a single word.

164

Like this, I came across many men who were so demanding, as if they wanted to handle me like a puppet. Every time while talking to them I felt dumbfounded.

It was quite frustrating, so somehow I said yes to an engineer. My father was happy as he was also tired of listening to relatives.

My father visited his family for the alliance. His father and brother too came to see me. Things went off well from both sides. However, after a few days, his family started bothering my father with dowry demands. My father had already promised to give enough, though I was not in favour of dowry. My mother said that it was the norm.

The engagement date was fixed. I started talking to my would-be fiancé over the phone. But suddenly, I heard his family demand something again, and my father was now unable to fulfil the demand. So I asked him to speak to his family. If he liked me, did money matter? But he said, "This is elder's matter, we children should not pitch in."

I was taken aback.

I said, "You might be a kid, but I am a grown-up. I cannot see my father taking unnecessary stress, who has done everything for me. So forgive me!"

The engagement was called off!

When I recall those days, I feel proud of myself, of being a woman, and of my parents who taught me to live life with self-esteem.

Let Them Go

There comes a series called Ahilya Bai on TV.

Whenever I get time, I watch it fondly. This serial is about the Holkar dynasty from Malwa state and focuses on the queen Ahilya Bai. Ahilyabai was a farmer's daughter who had been hard up. When she was eight years old, the king of Malwa, Malhar Rao Holkar selected her as a bride for his son. The reason was her strong character and wisdom which impressed the king. After marriage, the little Ahilya grew up in the palace, along with her husband Khande Rao Holkar. They played and studied together and learnt life skills. They developed a strong bonding with each other.

Gradually, she was disliked by many family members at the palace as she proved herself a source of sagacity, wisdom and compassion. The king grew fond of her which made people jealous.

In one of the episodes, they showed how queen Ahilya Bai and her husband Khande Rao Holkar had conflicts in their relationship.

They loved each other since childhood but a slight misunderstanding ruined their relationship and Khande

Rao's mother succeeded to convince him for a second marriage.

The day the second marriage got fixed Queen Ahilya Bai was not at the palace. Upon her return, she got to know about this news. She cried her heart out but didn't question her husband for making such a weird decision.

Her friend who was her caretaker too asked her why she was keeping quiet.

"Why don't you raise your voice, Ahilya? This is not fair." The caretaker asked.

While grieving she said she had no power to change someone's mind. This is out of her control. When Khande Rao made up his mind for another woman, it would be in vain to pull him back. Instead, she would let him go and accept the change.

I have the same feeling.

What is the use of holding a person back who is mentally not with me? I loved that person with all my heart, and it is only I who would feel the void once he was gone. He wouldn't because he didn't reciprocate the same love. If he had, he wouldn't go. Simple!

It hurts. At times, it becomes so unbearable that one feels like giving up.

But what can be done?

Loyalty can't be taught, love can't be forced and compassion can't be bought.

Emotions are Temporary

We cannot make a permanent decision for our temporary emotions........

Once I was in corporate training where the trainer was talking about email communication. He advised us to not write an email in aggression. If you receive a mail that makes you feel offended, don't respond to it immediately. Because a sudden surge of anger that you feel will appear in your reply. And it may cause a series of argumentative emails.

I loved this idea. In our day to day life, we experience all sorts of feelings. We feel emotional and become a cry baby. We get aggressive and want to end everything that seems to hurt. We are angry and take out our frustration on a wrong person or maybe in the wrong way.

Later, we are left with regrets and resentment. Words are bullets. Once they are shot, cannot be taken back. We live a life of repentance.

Are we so vulnerable?

Are we so hyper that we cannot control our temporary emotions?

Can't we become a little calm and think for a while before we react?

Ask yourself the above questions. I am sure you will find the answer - It is absolutely in your hand to regulate your feelings.

Let's be a little more sensible. Let's not allow ourselves to be carried away in the high tide of our emotions. We must know emotions are temporary. And we cannot make a permanent decision for our temporary emotions.

The Societal Pressure

Sharatchandra, a Bengali writer has written many novels. In the 19ᵗʰ century, he was known for his progressive and revolutionary thoughts.

I have been a huge fan of his writings. Every time (during my college days) I read his novel, I felt mesmerized.

To be true, I felt him in myself. I still remember how I used to scribble 'Sharat-Anshu' in my notebooks.

I recall an incident written in one of his novels that is still relevant.

There was a girl who was in love with a boy. She wanted to marry him but it was against her father's reputation. Her father was rich and was well known in the society.

The father convinced the daughter through emotional blackmail and with a heavy heart, the daughter got ready to marry the man from an affluent family whom her father had chosen.

Finally, the day of the wedding arrived. The father was spending a lot of money to make the wedding elegant. The arrangements were extraordinary. He was just throwing money to have everything perfect.

In a room, the daughter was sitting in her wedding dress. Her mother was beside her, watching the show through the window.

"Mom, look how much my father loves me. He is spending so much just to make my wedding grand and memorable." the daughter said.

And then, the mother retorted.

"Darling, your father doesn't love you. He loves his stature and prestige in the society. If he had loved you, he would have allowed you to marry the love of your life."

How contradictory each thought was! It's so true today as well. In the name of love, we cage our loved ones. We take the remote control of their life and snatch away their freedom.

Also, for many of us, social norms and our reputation in society is more important than our loved ones' life.

A friend tells me how passionate she had been about dance since her childhood. She wanted to make it her career. However, her engineer parents always compared her with the children who were good at academics. They were orthodox and could never consider singing and dancing as an art, in fact, they found it ugly. They could not understand that their daughter had a gift.

As a result, my friend was forced to pursue engineering which she never liked but she had to maintain her parents' reputation in society. She says she has lost herself. Something inside her has dropped away and she feels empty.

Cry or Celebrate?

I met Anmay on social media. He had been reading my blogs for long. And with time, he became a good friend to me.

Once he reached out to me with a personal problem.

As much as I knew him, I could say he is soft-hearted. An emotional person.

He told me that he had a girlfriend whom he truly loved. He dreamt of living with her. But the girl was not in love with him it seemed.

The more I knew about her, the more she seemed to be like a user. A selfish girl who was just using her boyfriend.

When she needed to travel, she called her boyfriend to buy tickets for her. When she was bored, she went out with him to have fun.

Money was not a problem. Anmay was well-settled in his job. He spent, she enjoyed. Her happiness was his happiness because he adored her.

He was so blind to her that he could never spare time to figure out if she really loved him. However, there were many signs that the girl showed which clearly revealed that she was just using him — sometimes for her expenses or other times, just to fill up her loneliness.

Whenever Anmay needed her, she had the excuses ready for not having time. Still, he could not understand.

Days, months and years went by. And one day, the girl announced that her parents were not ready for this marriage. She would marry the guy whom her parents had chosen for her — a guy who was richer and more successful, settled in Australia.

Within a short notice period, Anmay finally turned into her ex. She was gone - now happily married and settled in Australia.

But, Anmay was still lamenting in her memory. He was seeing a psychiatrist to overcome the depression but a simple thing he was not able to comprehend was that the girl was fake. He was fortunate enough that he didn't have to spend his whole life with a jerk. Staying alone is much better than being with someone who doesn't care about our emotions.

If he wanted to cry, he should have cried for his fate that he got to experience such a fake person in his life, not for the girl who only played with his emotions.

If he can still think this way, he will save himself from being an emotional fool and ruining his life further.

So, I say if someone has used you and left you at the end, you should celebrate it instead of crying for them. Because they are not worthy of you.

My Mom, My Inspiration

When I was in college, a cousin often used to tell me how beautiful my mother was when she was young. Even she told me I didn't inherit even a little bit of her looks.

These kind of statements left me in awe, though I always felt good hearing them. She is the woman who keeps herself up-to-date. I have hardly seen her messy, even at home. She has maintained herself, beautifully.

I recall an incident. I was 9–10 years old. She was once very sick and was not able to even walk. Her face had grown pale. Dad was himself treating her. But later, he decided to visit a senior doctor whose clinic was 20 kilometers away from our place.

In that sickness too, my mom gathered all her energy to put on a nice silk saree and little makeup with red lipstick.

I was bewildered.

I accompanied her to the car. To my surprise, she was looking so fresh.

No matter how sick or depressed she feels with her age and the circumstances around her, she has not shown a sign to the world. Nobody can guess if she is going through some hardships.

I truly feel inspired by her. Of course, I am not as maintained as her but I too visit doctors or any other person with grace. From her, I learned, yes appearance matters.

Physical beauty is not everything. The most important thing is how one carries oneself. This is what I learned from her.

She is the person who knows the difference between spending and living life. I believe this is the thing that keeps her going.

Another life skill I learned from her is resilience.

This is what I like most about her. She doesn't give up. No matter how hard life seems, she doesn't lose her hopes. She is persistent.

In our daily conversation, whenever she finds me dismayed, she will tell me the quotes from Geeta. She persuades me to believe in God and motivates me to face the obstacles of life.

"When Lord Rama and Krishna suffered so much on this earth, we are just human beings," she says.

She has been very positive about life. She believes in the law of attraction and always keeps the book "The Secret" beside her.

She commits to everything wholly that she finds worth. In her tough times, when things seemed going awry and she was unable to find solace, I saw her recite the holy book Shri Ramcharitmanas loudly. She says while reciting it, the negativity seeps away and she is able to restore herself back. Though I could not comprehend this faith, I admire her to find her ways.

While growing up, the best tip for parenting I learnt from her was giving freedom to children. And I am really grateful to her for this. She gave me freedom – freedom to analyse things on my own. She let me decide what was wrong and right for me. She never gave me her beliefs, nor forced me to follow anything blindly. It was completely up to me how I reached any conclusion.

I remember an incident related to this.

After the demise of my best friend, I went through a bout of internal disarray and lost my faith in God. I had become an atheist. During those days, my parents came to see me in Bangalore. They stayed with me for a few days. One evening when I returned from the office, my mother expressed her desire to visit a temple nearby and requested me to accompany her.

I accompanied her to the temple but denied to enter the temple premise. I told her that I didn't believe in those stones. She, though being a religious woman, didn't compel me to visit the temple. She didn't make any effort to persuade me to change my mind but asked me to stay outside and wait for her. She gave me space and time to figure out if I was correct in my behaviour.

She never encouraged me to be a part of the crowd.

That was wonderful. That helped me develop my own thoughts in later years.

For my writing, many people have asked me how could I think out of the box. And I say, the credit goes to my mother.

The Power of Writing

When I think of my childhood, I see the image of an adamant little girl who wanted to resolve her problems in her own way. She wanted to change the system by voicing out. If she got the chance to speak up, she spoke her mind without fear. But when there seemed no such possibilities, she expressed herself on paper.

I remember many such incidents where she made efforts to keep her points by writing. Writing a letter to the Prime Minister is one of them.

She grew studious and at a very young age, somehow she had developed a belief that study is more important than anything in this world. Maybe, reading brilliant articles about great people inspired her to think so.

She was emotionally attached to some of her teachers who always helped her in her studies to the best of their abilities.

She was in 5th grade when she suddenly felt that mathematics is not her cup of tea. Somehow, she started losing interest in the subject and struggled to solve a simple mathematical problem.

Then her school teacher, whom she forced to become her home tutor, helped her get her interest back. He was not only brilliant in mathematics but also he possessed the art of explaining difficult things in a simple language.

Learning with him, in a span of a year, she got hold of the subject. She was elated when she got the highest marks in the class. She was immensely grateful to him and wished to continue learning in the coming years as well.

However, her happiness couldn't last long. The teacher got a transfer order and soon, he was to change school and shift to a different town.

After hearing this news, the little Anshu went to pieces, but she had not learned to give up. She wanted to have her teacher in the school at any cost, though she had no clue about how to resolve it.

"This is an order from the government, Anshu. I can't do anything. Don't worry, you will do well in life," The teacher consoled her with a solemn expression when she asked him to stay back with tears in her eyes.

"Well! If this is a government order, then let me speak to the government itself", she thought to herself and left without uttering a word.

And then, she wrote a letter to the Prime Minister, explaining everything to him about how education is important in one's life and what role a good teacher plays in the student's life. Further, she explained how good her teacher was and how much she was going to lose in his absence.

Sounds silly? Yes, it does. Even the postman, whom she handed over the letter, chuckled looking at the address on top of the envelope:

Atal Bihari Vajpayee,

Prime Minister of India,

New Delhi, India.

She desperately waited for the Prime Minister's response for long. Days, months and a year went by, the teacher got transferred and gradually, she too forgot about the letter as she found another brilliant teacher by her side.

There is one more such incident. A new teacher joined the school. He taught social science. He was a bright young man and was preparing for civil services. This time she was in 8th grade. A teenager who was impressed by this young man's teaching. He has all the answers to satisfy her curiosity.

After a few months, the teacher had some conflicts with the school management. Probably, his popularity among students in such a short time was not liked by the head of the school. So, he was replaced by another teacher who was old and dull. He was asked to teach in junior classes.

The management head was very strict. He had such an intimidating personality. No student had the courage to speak with him, even Anshu too was afraid of him. So this time too, she took the help of writing.

She collected the guts to write a letter to him. In the letter, she politely requested him to send the teacher back to the class. She handed over the letter to him with a shivering hand.

To her surprise, the next day, the young bright man was back in her class.

With these two incidents, I realised the power of writing at that time. If one can put one's feelings or opinion well in words, no matter how tough the situation is, the matter can be conveyed. The consequences may not be exemplary but one would be surely heard.

The Patrons

A friend is highly educated. She has studied law and done many courses, like a foreign language, yoga etc.

But her biggest disappointment is that she doesn't have any passion to follow. No hobby to pursue.

She often compares herself with me. She finds me fortunate that I have writing skills. I can give words to whatever I feel, see or experience.

"You got a knack", she says to me.

But you know I find her best. Best among all. She is an observer, an admirer. She is an avid reader. She is sensitive and can feel others' pain.

She reads all my blogs on social media and can immediately sense if it is related to me or anyone else. She has this ability. I don't think everyone has. Even a writer, poet or artist lacks this sensitivity sometimes.

She is not good at Hindi but still, she reads my poems and tries to take a dive into their thoughts. Not all of us can do it if we are not familiar with the language.

Imagine, if everyone is a painter, who will admire your painting?

If everyone is a writer, who will be a reader to go through your content and applaud them?

If all are silent, who will be there to scream at your success?

So for me, she is that admirer. She is a brilliant guide, who can show a path to people in their darkness.

Sometimes brightness is hidden. We need special eyes to see beauty.

Not everyone is blessed with some skills. But not everyone is born having nothing.

Some people have the quality beyond all the qualities. Sometimes, even the noblest of things and greatest of artists are nothing compared to a human being who has nothing but life to offer. Poetry need not always be in the form of words, anything from cooking to driving to cleaning can be done in a poetic way. And living a poetic life is a much bigger and more beautiful thing than being officially known for some passion.

My Journey as a Single Mother

I am a single mother - Living in 2022 with people's mindset of 1922.

My status is a big deal.

Divorce is considered ugly which I got to know after going through this. People either lose respect or pity me. Some people try to take me easy.

It's even a huge "Aww" moment for kind people when they get to know my status. They show concern and feel sad.

All this amazes me to the hilt. I look at myself -from top to bottom - I find no change. I am the same woman now as I was before my divorce. I don't feel anything ugly about myself. In fact, I feel like a conqueror.

Still, I face these "aww" moments every now and then. I keep receiving advice and questions, such as, I should go for remarriage. Life is too long. How would I live alone? Or even, how would I control my sexual urges? I must find someone.

Our country is full of advisors. They are always ready to give us advice. Free of cost! These advisors are so insensitive that they are unable to think if their advice can bruise someone's sentiments.

Some people are unable to control their curiosity. They can ask anything to anyone anywhere. Sex is overrated. According to people here, a man or woman may die without it. I really don't understand this mindset. I wonder how ignorant they are. I wonder how much they are trapped in worldly affairs that they are unable to think beyond them.

The story does not end here.

If I am talking to a man nicely, I'm immediately suspected - might be, I am looking for some benefits or a relationship out of that. I wonder if this mentality can be ever changed. I am single and I know how to carry myself with dignity, grace and self-control. How can I explain it to them? I don't think I would ever be able to explain, so I just smile.

I live in Bangalore - one of the biggest cities in India. However, here too, people tried to take me for granted just because I am a single mother. And I have no man at home to protect me. When I raised my voice and did not let them take me easy, they reached the conclusion that I was arrogant and gossiped that my arrogance was the reason for my failed marriage.

Someone found me the best woman in the world and wished to marry me but he said his parents wouldn't accept me because of my status. Again, I had a smile.

In our society, marital status is a medium to define a person. A divorced woman is probably considered to be without a soul. I think this is the reason why I get the advice on remarriage.

Can't I live alone? Is it so important to have a man to continue life? I don't think so. I am not that vulnerable. I know how to take my steps. I love to be myself.

So my question to them is - Can't they stop demeaning or pitying a single woman? Can't they admire her for being strong and walking out of a toxic relationship?

I wish people in our country could understand a few simple things. Marriage or having a partner is not the ultimate goal of life. Not having a partner doesn't make one less. Being single doesn't prove one vulnerable.

If a woman can walk out of her marriage and find her own way, then she must be considered the strongest. She can establish an empire for herself and live a life beyond one's imagination. Also, she might be an owner of a pure soul that could not be safeguarded in this cruel world and therefore, she had to take a harsh step.

Divorce is not ugly, being a coward and letting oneself suffer is ugly.

We are Chained

I met this woman while travelling to Mumbai on a train.

It was almost a 24 hours long journey. I was carrying the book "Brida" written by Paulo Coelho to pass time. While I was engrossed in reading, I noticed that this woman sitting across me was staring at me. Or at the book. I can't say.

I lifted my head to have an eye contact and then we exchanged a smile. She looked sophisticated in her white cotton designer saree with blue borders. She was in her early 60s.

I suddenly felt affectionate towards her.

"I have read a few books written by Paulo Coelho. I liked them a lot. However, what you are reading is still unknown to me. How do you find it?" She asked.

"Spellbinding! I am feeling drawn towards this woman named Brida." I responded with a smile.

And then she got up and came to my seat. I folded my legs and she sat beside me.

"I would like to know why are you feeling drawn towards this woman." She asked.

And then, I explained to her how wise and ambitious Brida was. How she explored things in life and at times, how lonely and miserable did she feel in a world full of people.

"If someone has made up their mind to explore the world and life, they have to be on a roller coaster. At times, they can feel miserable and face ordeals, but they are the ones who taste life in the true sense." She said.

"Have you had the taste of life", I asked out of the blue.

"I wish I could but I got trapped by worldly affairs. Got married early, had unlimited sex and reproduced three children. I got so occupied with my responsibilities, that I couldn't spare a minute to look back and check what the young Vasudha actually wanted. By the way, my name is Vasudha Aryan." She answered introducing herself.

"Ah! Sounds interesting. Would you be able to share what the young Vasudha wanted?" I blinked my eyes with curiosity.

"The young Vasudha wanted to explore everything that came her way. Without getting conditioned by society. Deep down, she did not like to have children and waste her life nurturing them. She wanted to be a free soul who could wander at her own pace. Do you know fakir? How do they live? With zero worries! They have nothing to lose, they just go with the flow of life. They roam here, there and everywhere. I wanted to be that fakir and live life with that ease."

"Then why didn't you do that?" I couldn't stop myself from asking.

"Do you think our society would allow us to live like that? We are conditioned everywhere. Our future is written the moment we are born. And when we gradually develop our conscience, the list of dos and don'ts is given to us. We are compelled to follow the rules of the society, or else we are discarded. The fear of getting discarded is so intense that hardly anyone can dare to become like Brida. Becoming Brida is not easy you know", she said.

Our lunch had arrived. She went back to her seat to have it and I kept on thinking how conditioned we are, how chained we are. Though life is ours, still we are not supposed to live it the way we want. I thought of my graduation days and recalled a line of Rousseau which had impacted me most during those days. 'Man is born free but everywhere is in chains.' Had said Rousseau.

The Idea of Marriage

Marriage is an imprisonment.

Yes, marriage is a fine cage to lock you forever - with a person whom you may love or not. Still, you are bound to make love. That's the ugliest thing about marriage.

And then, making love becomes a duty - a means to fulfil your partner's desire.

Marriage cuts down your freedom. It will cut your wings and make you handicapped. Once you are married, you are not supposed to make decisions on your own. You have to prioritise your partner, children, family, community, society, priest (who tied the knot) and then, your number comes at the end.

You are finished!

There are millions of people who are depressed being in the marriage. There are many psychological problems that take place after one gets married. The psychologists will keep on giving you advice and making money out of that, but they will never tell you the root cause. If they reveal the root cause, their job is finished.

They are smart, we are fools!

Osho says we are humans. Our likes and dislikes change with time. Today I like you, tomorrow I may not. But still, I am forced to live with you, just because I am married to you.

This is utterly foolish!

If you have noticed marriages, you will find this is the most convenient relationship to take someone for granted. One dominates another - One surrenders to another.

In a true sense, it's just a relationship between a master and a slave.

Maybe, this was the reason why Tagore gave a new concept of marriage where a couple decides to live separately after their wedding. They believe - if they stay together, the freshness of their love will fade.

I appreciate that!

Awareness in Your Children

I taught my child many things at a very young age.

He learnt about sexual abuse and menstruation at the age of 3. When I shared this with some people, I was highly denounced.

"How could you tell such a small kid that you bleed? Isn't it scary? How could you introduce him to sanitary napkins calling them mummy's diapers? Isn't it disgusting?" I was bombarded with countless such questions.

However, it didn't matter to me.

I taught him what I felt must be taught. And I noticed its positive outcomes as well. Every month, during my period, he understands that his mother is feeling weak due to bleeding, she should be in rest and he should not be troubling her.

To be honest, it's a big relief!

A few days ago, he has started his offline school. This is the first time in the last two years, that he is away from me for six to seven hours every day. So as a mother, I was a little worried.

On the first day, I went to drop him off at the school. After parking my vehicle, we had to walk around a hundred meters inside the school compound. The crowd was huge inside and outside the school as it had reopened after Covid.

While walking along with him, suddenly a thought came to my mind — what if he encounters sexual abuse in my absence? I got goosebumps. I had taught him about it long back. Does he still remember? I wanted to check.

"Sweetie, tell me something. Can anyone touch your private part - your teacher, friend, big kids or the cleaning aunty in the washroom?" I asked lowering my voice, almost whispering, as so many people were around.

"No, No, No.... Nobody can touch." He replied loudly.

It was so loud that a woman standing ahead turned back to find from where the voice was coming. And we exchanged smiles without explaining anything.

However, at this moment I felt proud of this tiny creature. He seemed to be so mature and determined, well aware of the cruel world.

The world, we are living in, is not safe for some of us. Irrespective of gender, one can be sexually harassed anytime.

We cannot be there to safeguard our children every time, but let's make them aware of such a heinous act and prepare them for that. They must learn to voice out and we must learn to train them how to deal with the problem instead of getting depressed.

193

Let's Know the True Meaning of Life

In one of my previous organizations, there was a manager. He was very rude. He didn't know how to treat and greet his employees. He considered them like his cattle. A person admired by him today might be screwed up tomorrow.

Uncertainty everywhere!

Due to his position, he was powerful. Nobody had the guts to oppose him. He was a dictator. Probably a tyrant.

Everyone had respect for him. But that respect came out of fear. They knew raising voices against him will spoil their career. They were quiet. They pretended to be humble in front of him.

But there was no one who did not speak ill behind his back. He was cursed every day. He was disdained by everyone.

What amazed me most was his unawareness. He was unaware of this hatred and remained proud of his position and power. He could never realize the true essence of life.

Well, you can be powerful. You can be stronger than others. You can dominate the world but you cannot reside in someone's heart. You will not be cherished once you leave the world. You may not get anyone wishing you "Rest In Peace".

Do you ever figure out the purpose of your life? Do you ever feel blessed to have so many things and think of using them for others' welfare?

Please think once.

Why Don't We Take an Easy Route?

Life is difficult. For some of us, it's ugly. However, many times, a question arises in my mind - Why don't we opt for an easy route?

We all dream to soar high. We aspire to become/have this and that. This is absolutely fine. Life must have a purpose. Without a goal, it becomes monotonous.

But do we ever measure our capability before setting the goal?

I am not so good at mathematics, still, I want to become an engineer. I study hard, coping with calculations. But how long can I survive like this? One day, a mathematician will dump me somewhere in the race and I will be blaming life for how difficult it is. Life did not give me what I wanted.

Wish, I had gone for something I was good at and had placed myself in some good position. Life would not seem this difficult. Right?

This is just one example. If you notice around, you will find yourself trapped everywhere. And there is nobody to be blamed for. You are responsible for your situation.

You aspire more than your ability. You compete with everyone whom you find successful. You strive for unrealistic things. And later, you blame life and God.

I know life is miserable. It's not easy. I still say you can make it easier by being a little realistic. You don't have to compare yourself with others. You don't have to compete with everyone. You must know your level and capacity. Be positive, appreciate others and learn to be yourself. Don't forget you are unique. Try to find out your uniqueness and polish it as long as it becomes presentable to the world.

Have Faith and Patience

I have been regularly watching a TV show about the Saint Sai Baba of Shirdi.

He says to all his devotees to have Shraddha (faith) and Saburi (patience).

Initially, I could not comprehend its importance. But with time, I realised how relevant it was. When I look at my past, I find it a complete mess. Things were definitely going downhill but my restlessness, despair and impatience made it worse. With the noisy mind, I was not able to find a way to discover how to deal with the situation.

I had become impatient and edgy which made my life more miserable. I had considered myself the most unfortunate soul.

I wish I had learned to have faith and patience at that time. My life would have been better or at least, my mental health would have been less affected.

However, at present, whenever I feel hopeless or things seem going awry, I remind myself to stay positive. I believe in the universe, God and the law of attraction. I try my best to keep my faith alive. Because faith gives us hope. A hope that life would get better. Things will change for good.

If my faith seems to weaken, I write to myself stating that it is just a testing phase. I tell the universe no matter how hard you hit me, I will stay strong. My resilience will melt you one day.

Now I believe that nothing is impossible in life. It's all about time. Give time to everything if you want to bring change. Keep making efforts with lots of patience, and have faith in God, the universe and yourself.

Nothing is permanent. Your bad days will surely end.

How I Changed My Life

Many people have asked me how I changed my life. They want to know how I evolved stronger and more confident and how I could get rid of my tough times. It did not happen in a day or week but it took time. My constant efforts to learn about life helped me grow stronger.

I adopted two methods to change my life.

By believing in the Universe.

After reading the book *"The Secret"* written by Rhonda Byrne, I learnt how the universe acts for everyone and how powerful it is.

At times, I was depressed and wanted to quit. Looking at my difficulties, I had become an atheist. I had stopped praying to God.

But when I got to read this book and placed an order to the universe for a peaceful life, slowly and slowly my life started changing.

How do you place an order online and then forget about it? You don't doubt about its arrival. You believe the product will come to you. Likewise, I too believed in the universe. Maybe, a little late, but I will get what I have asked for. And my faith worked out.

The universe is very kind to each of us.

By taking responsibility for my miseries.

I realised that no one is responsible for my miseries but it is me. Imploring others to be nice to me is worthless. Blaming them for my difficult situation is a crime.

If I can't take action to rescue myself from a difficult situation, how can I expect others to help?

If I allow people to interfere in my life and steal my mental peace, I will definitely lead a miserable life.

When I realised the above, I disconnected myself from all unworthy things, situations and people. I took ownership of my life and the responsibility of keeping myself healthy and fine.

And then, my life changed.

Hope this helps you too.

The Value of Money

My parents came to stay with us for some time. They are very concerned about me and my child as I am a single mother.

I had been jobless for the whole year in 2020. This was the year when I had to face financial hardship. Being in the private sector, losing a job is considered normal. During this year, I realised one must have some financial security if he/she is working in corporates. One must be ready to face unemployment anytime as there is no job security here.

Hence, I have become a bit careful when it comes to spending money. I make sure there is no wastage or unnecessary shopping.

However, I am trying my best to give a good life to my child. Along with that, I am teaching him life lessons as well as I can. At this early age, I believe, he has learnt enough to value money.

So during this visit, my mother wanted to buy a new carpet for our living room, considering the existing one old. I was telling her it was not required as of now, but she was still insisting on buying one.

This six-year-old boy was in the other room and heard the word "buying". He immediately asked me what Nani (he calls my mother "Nani") wanted to buy.

"Carpet," I said expecting him to tell me the colour for the new carpet.

He is generally interested in getting new things, he even likes to have new, colourful bed sheets. But to my surprise, his response was quite strange this time.

"Why does Nani want to buy a new carpet? We already have one and we are happy with whatever we have. But Nani doesn't understand. Isn't it, Mumma? Tell her not to waste money." he said firmly.

I was touched. I didn't know when this little munchkin grew up and became this understanding. I just pray to this universe that he should become a good, sensitive and kind-hearted person. The world is in need of good human beings.

There have been many times when my child demands something that his friends are having. He insists on buying that and I am capable to buy, but I still refuse. As a parent, this is my responsibility to provide him with a sense of purpose. So I explain to him that one cannot have everything. At times, I take him to show the poor children who don't even get proper meals. But they don't compare their lives with ours and therefore, live in peace. This way he is not only learning gratitude, empathy and self-satisfaction but also, he is overcoming the feeling of avarice and comparison. He is learning to accept rejections too.

Setting Boundaries

I had not set boundaries with a few people in my life due to fear of losing them.

And the consequences had been heart wrenching. I had given them the right to crush me, talk ill about me or belittle me.

I couldn't maintain a distance from them as I had my own insecurities and vulnerabilities. Every time, being with them, I felt dismayed. Life seemed the real bitch and the only thing I wanted was to quit.

I couldn't take any action which could make the relationship healthier that could have safeguarded my mental peace.

However, when I set the boundaries, things drastically changed. The fear of losing people became the least concern to me as I realised that having people who are a threat to my mental peace is futile.

Those people too understood my worth. They learnt to respect my self-esteem. They didn't bother me if I wanted to have my privacy and space.

I have learnt in my life that it is worthless to struggle to have people. The one, who has to stay with you, will stay with you. The one, who has to leave, will leave no matter how hard you try to keep them around. Setting up a boundary helped me get quality people as friends. They understood me well and gave me space too. They are definitely less in number but high in intelligence.

Setting boundaries is not only necessary for your own good but for the relationship too. Be it your siblings, parents, friends, spouse etc. You need to set boundaries with each of them.

And then, you will live peacefully forever.

Attention Needed

"Please hold me, Sweetie", I asked my baby at night as soon as we went to bed.

"Nowadays you don't come closer, so I don't hold you." He said in a firm voice.

I was taken aback. I didn't expect such a statement from him. He is just six. However, I could sense where it was coming from.

I immediately kissed him on the forehead and apologized. I cuddled him close and talked to him for some time. And then, he fell asleep.

In that darkness, holding him in my arms, I realised how careless I had become over the last few days. Many times, he came to me to show or tell something, and I responded to him carelessly, without listening to him properly. Either I was occupied with my office work or blogging on social media.

I was immediately filled with regret and guilt conscious. I didn't pay attention to him. I did take care of him but at times, I failed to listen to him.

And here was he, feeling neglected. Ignored and disappointed.

Tears rolled down my cheeks. I whispered '*I love you*' to him while he was in deep sleep.

Be it any kind of relationship, attention is needed. It is the foundation of the relationship. How much time we spend with our loved ones doesn't matter. What matters is how much quality time we spend with them. How much we make them feel that they are heard is the most important ingredient of a successful relationship.

So when you are with your loved ones, make sure you are solely with them. This will help you and your loved ones connect emotionally.

I am going to do the same, would you?

A Way of Life that Makes Us a Better Person

I will give two examples that happened recently:

I was talking to an acquaintance over the phone who told me about something bad that someone did to him and he felt very hurt.

You will be amazed to know that he had done the same thing to me six months ago and I had felt equally hurt. You will be more surprised to know that he remembered the incident but he was sure that it was not to hurt me.

This irked me a lot. However, I didn't say anything, and after a few minutes, we disconnected the call.

After that, I kept on thinking about how people don't realize it at all even if they go through the same.

Another incident occurred on social media.

I read a blog that was defending the actress Rhea Chakravarti who was suspected to be involved in the murder of the actor Sushant Singh Rajput. I am one of Sushant's fans who was badly affected by his sudden demise and logically went through every small detail related to Sushant's death through media, people's perceptions, interviews, Rhea's changing statements, etc.

I believe if Rhea is not a culprit, she can't be innocent too. This is solely my opinion and I can be wrong too.

So again, this write-up in Rhea's favour irked me. I couldn't keep calm and wrote my comment. The writer bashed me as he had a different opinion.

So, how to become a better person?

We must learn to stay calm as I always suggest to my online readers. However, I had miserably failed in the second example.

The world has varieties of people - with varieties of opinions and mindsets.

You can't change them no matter how wrong they are. If you try, you will lose your mental peace only.

To become a better person, you must learn to keep your opinion to yourself. And also, learn to ignore people. Speak less, and shun arguments, conflicts and confrontations with people as much as you can. Because they are toxic, malignant and do not help anyone. At times, it's difficult but accept that you have no choice.

Learn to move on! Keep yourself occupied with something that interests you.

Increase Your Immunity

I often tell my online readers how to be brave to face the difficulties of life. At some point in time, I literally wanted to quit. I was so dismayed and depressed.

However, I could make efforts to change the circumstances of my life. I walked out of my failed marriage and went for a divorce.

And now, I am at peace.

I have this belief that we are ourselves responsible for our miseries. Why can't one take action to rescue oneself from a tough situation? If I could do it, why can't others?

However, with time, I realised that it was not an easy step. I had the courage to break the relationship. I am bold enough to face the consequences of my action. But not everyone is the same. Not everyone has got the strength to take extreme steps.

I get several messages from readers stating that they have no courage to change the circumstances of their life and therefore, they are suffering.

I understand it better now.

So I want to tell all such people — if you can't change the circumstances, then increase your immunity to face them. Do you know there are many diseases which can't be cured and the doctors advise us only to increase our immunity to avoid them?

Dear readers, life is beautiful. Don't think of ending it just because you are stuck with your miseries. If you cannot come out of them, then at least be strong enough to face them. Find ways to take care of yourself in those odd circumstances. Remember that we can't control bad situations from happening to us but we can learn how to handle it and live with it.

Be a warrior and conquer the world.

Out of Comfort Zone

My child had to present 'The Thought of The Day' in his class. I felt so proud of teaching him the below lines:

"Life is too short to regret. So live your life to the fullest."

I get messages from my readers where they admire me for being independent and capable to make my decisions. They consider me their inspiration.

It feels good but when they mention that they are suffering in life and are unable to come out of a toxic relationship, it really hurts. They wonder how I could do it and why they couldn't.

They couldn't because they valued social norms more than their own being. They cared about the world more than themselves. And from here, their miseries started.

They couldn't understand that an empty cup pours out nothing. They cared about others and remained empty forever. This emptiness gave them dissatisfaction, depression, and sadness. They have been afraid of challenges and hesitated to come out of their comfort zone. They never tried to look beyond the well in which they had been dwelling for years.

They never trusted the sun which could be a bright hope for them.

Life is full of shit. But trust me, 75% of that are self-created. We can easily fix them by collecting a little courage. But the problem is we don't listen to our hearts, we don't want to make efforts, and we don't dare to take risks. Instead, we expect some magic to happen and change everything which is impossible.

Remember, nothing comes free in life. If you want to achieve something, you have to pay for that. Either you pay through courage, effort or by sacrificing a little.

For all this, you have to take risks. In the book "Who will cry when you die", Robin Sharma says,

"On your deathbed, it will not be all the risks you took that you will regret the most. Rather, what will fill your heart with the greatest amount of regret and sadness will be all those risks that you didn't take, all those opportunities you didn't seize and all those fears you didn't face."

The Qualities that I Want My Child to Imbibe

After picking him up from the school, on the way, he expressed his desire to eat chips.

I took him to a shop where he bought two different packets of his favourite chips.

He was elated.

As we were walking towards our vehicle parked nearby, we saw a child sitting on the pavement. In his dirty, torn clothes he looked miserable, which melted my heart. His parents were probably those labourers filling the holes and puddles on the road.

I politely asked my child to give a packet to him. He seemed hesitant to share but soon what he said made my day.

"Mumma, let's make others happy.", Saying this he quickly handed over the packet.

At this moment, I felt so proud of him. A little compassion and kindness which I always tried to instil in my child were apparent to me.

Sometimes, he complains that his friends don't involve him in their group. They boycott him. He feels left out and lonely. I understand his emotions as he is just six. However, I have been teaching him to not give a damn to people who don't care about our emotions.

"Be brave and move on." This is the mantra he is learning slowly and trying to implement instead of shedding tears.

This is another trait I want to develop in my child. Don't whine but move on. Be yourself. Accept the circumstances and live with them if they can't be changed. The bottom line is, 'what cannot be cured must be endured'.

Recently, in his school, he had a session of creative writing where he was asked to write about a wish that he wanted the fairy to grant.

"I will ask the fairy to make me intelligent so that all the teachers and kids will love me." He wrote with a few spelling mistakes.

I was amazed as I had not expected it from him. A six years old boy craves toy cars, guns and fun activities but here is my boy thinking differently. I immediately thanked the universe for directing him to the right path.

Though I don't find him interested in reading as of now, I always pray for him to become an avid reader. I myself read in front of him as I have heard that the children imitate. I keep lecturing him about the importance of books and how life-changing they can be.

The Responsibility of a Doctor

Amidst many childhood memories, I would like to recall one with immense pride which I did not understand at that time. I think I was too small to comprehend its impact and relevance.

I would be about 7–8 year old. As a doctor, my father was practising vigorously. He had earned a lot of name and fame in his career. He was earning well and was also serving poor people free of cost when needed. For him, someone's life was more important than anything else. My native place was a small place which lacked doctors at that time. His patients came even from remote areas.

He was so dedicated to his profession that he didn't bother about the time when he got a call from the patients. He went to see patients in remote villages at midnight if someone came to call him.

There was no road at that time and mostly he had to walk. He was handsome and physically fit.

So one night he was going to attend a call accompanied by a middle-aged man whose old father was suffering from diarrhoea. He urgently needed to be on IV fluids.

As they walked down the alley beside the empty fields surrounded by rosewood trees and looked out over the widely spread darkness, everything seemed calm and serene in the torch light. After walking around 800 meters in that calmness, they heard a terrifying noise. Before my father could think of anything and be careful, some gunmen suddenly appeared in front of them.

It was quite a scary situation. They were dacoits. One of them came forward and snatched my father's wristwatch, gold ring and wallet showing him a revolver. He was sweating out of fear.

Suddenly, the leader of the gang recognised my father in the torch light and shouted at his folk stating,

"Leave him, he is our doctor. Let him go."

He then beckoned my father to leave. They even returned the things to him.

When my father came back home in the morning and narrated the whole story to my mom, she was shivering out of fear. She cried and strictly restricted him from attending such calls at night.

My father didn't say anything.

Two days later, at night, again, someone knocked on our main gate.

"Doctor Sahab! Please visit my house. My wife is very sick." We heard.

At that time, I used to sleep with my parents. My father quickly got up and reached the veranda to talk to that person. After discussing the condition of the patient, probably he felt the need to attend to the patient.

So he started getting ready.

And here, in bed, my mother was fuming. When he was about to leave, my mother stood in front of him, blocking his way. I could clearly see the tears rolling down her face.

"Please let me go." My father said.

"No, I won't let you risk your life. Why can't you think of me and your children? If anything happens to you, what shall we do?" Mom asked holding the door tenaciously with both of her hands.

"Just imagine yourself standing at the gate of a doctor's house and begging the doctor to attend me because I am sick and I need urgent treatment. But the doctor doesn't turn up to see me. How would you feel? Wouldn't you curse the doctor and his degree?" he asked slowly and calmly.

My mother quietly drifted away from the door and let him go. He nudged her shoulders gently assuring her that he would be back soon.

Mother couldn't close her eyes even for a second until he was back around 5:30 am. Her worries kept her awake all night but the best thing I felt was that she could understand the responsibilities of a doctor and never became an obstacle in his work. And my father could keep his personal and professional life separate.

Past is Nothing But a Story

I have received several messages from the readers where they shared their pain of not being able to forget the past. The memory of the past is excruciating which is not letting them accept the present. And this way they are spoiling their present as well.

When I was in a marriage, my husband was everything to me. After the divorce, somehow I was still attached to him. Whenever I met him, my eyes got wet.

However, the relationship was already dead and I needed to accept my present without him as soon as possible. It was difficult but I didn't let it become an impossible task.

I have always been a very pragmatic, practical person with an awareness of how to overcome the situation. I started working on myself. I created the willingness to step out of the bondage of the past and live my life to the fullest. I trusted my capabilities and established my own world where I felt emotionally secure.

A few friends and most of my readers on social media are close to my heart. Some of them became my solace. Interacting with them, I found the purpose of my life.

I started keeping myself busy with one or other things and as a single mother, being occupied became my destiny. The life of a single mother is always tough but I tried getting tougher.

It's been three years since I got separated from my husband and a lot of changes have taken place in my life. Most of them were positive and because of my constant efforts, I was able to accept my present with grace.

At times, my mother feels sorry for my divorce. And I often need to convince her about how much I am healed now. I really don't look back and regret anything. In fact, I feel proud to have a story through which I look forward to bringing change in other's life.

What is gone is gone. It's absolutely futile to waste time and energy thinking about that. Instead, I would suggest you look forward. Look forward to having a better future, and make efforts to make your dreams come true.

Don't curse your past, fate or anyone but accept them as a memory — be it good or bad. Know that you cannot change them but you can definitely restart your life as I did with my child.

Parenting at Stake

My sister recently shifted to a new apartment in Mumbai.

My 10-year-old niece was quite excited about its playground and large swimming pool. So once everything settled down, my sister started sending her down to play with other kids.

In a few days only, the niece started complaining that the children have formed a clique. They boycott her and she feels lonely.

A few kids talk to her nicely only when their group is not present. If they don't have enough kids to play with, they involve her.

One day she came home saddened. My sister asked her several times if she was fine but she kept quiet and headed to her room.

After a few minutes, my sister went to check and found her sobbing amidst the pillows. When she asked the reason for this, she told that the kids often bully her by calling her a dog.

"Your face looks like a dog." They say.

I was aghast when I heard this over the phone. I spoke to my niece and asked her not to give a damn to those kids. I encouraged her to read books. I asked her not to feel lonely. Because being alone is much better than being in bad company. But she didn't say a word.

I could feel her pain as I myself experienced this in one of my previous jobs. The colleagues often left me alone for no reason. If I ever tried to join their group, I felt outcast and unwanted. Their behaviour was strange to me as I was unable to find the reason for this rejection. I couldn't take it and felt immensely hurt.

Anyways, they were adults but here these are children. Children are known for their innocence but here, I heard they do groupism. They do politics. At such early age, they have learnt to bully.

From where are they learning such things? A friend says they are learning from their parents. This shocked me even more.

What sort of people their parents are? What are they teaching their kids?

We are living in a world where we are already lacking empathy. After ten years when these kids turn into adults, they will be an add-on to this scarcity.

I am dismayed. Really!

As parents, it's our responsibility to teach compassion to our children. We need to sensitize the kids about being compassionate, being inclusive. I do it, I often explain to my child how to behave, why not to hurt others and how to live life with kindness. What he doesn't like for himself, he must not do to others. I teach him because I have suffered in my life. At that time, I hated those people and I don't want anyone to hate my child for the same reason.

I wish all of us to take this sensitive topic into consideration. Because we adults too suffer from groupism, bullying and politics.

A Life Advice

A young man reached out to me for life advice.

He was 28 years old. He wanted to change his whole life and image in front of people, but he felt that he should have done this in his early 20s. Now he was afraid of being judged by people if he tried to change his life.

I understood his apprehension and fear. At some point in time, we all wish for the same but the fear of being judged doesn't let us work on ourselves.

I expressed my wish to this young man as well and wrote to him as below:

I wish I was your age — 28.

I could have corrected many of the mistakes that I made in my early 20s.

Probably I wouldn't have suffered so much in my failed marriage. I would have worked on myself much before and made a decision. As a result, I would have been more composed. I would have been free from panic attacks and mood swings.

I would have worked on my career too and probably had gone for civil services.

But 28 is gone and now I am in my 30s. I can't change my past. I can't go back and fix the issues of my life.

However, I have all the possibilities to improve my present and future. If the possibilities are not there, I can create them. And then, I can regrow.

I don't sit idle. In fact, I can't. I have my ups and downs — bright and gloomy days. And I make sure that I work on myself at least during the bright days.

I don't care about people. Who the hell are they to notice the change in me? However, I feel elated when they notice the change in me. Recently, a relative asked me on WhatsApp how I was doing. I understood what exactly she wanted to know. People are curious to know about my life after divorce. I answered her like a badass saying that I was relishing life. And she said she noticed it too, looking at my WhatsApp status. And this is true as well. I was not this vibrant before.

So you see, I am noticed. And it doesn't bother me.

Another relative recently advised my mother to go for my remarriage. My mother told them that Anshu is no more a little girl. She knows how to make decisions about her life.

Everyone is observing the change in me. They are dumbfounded to see how carefree a woman is, even after facing the most difficult phase of her life.

226

So I would say to you as well — Do what you like. Don't seek anyone's attention, approval or admiration for things that you do. If you want to bring change to your personality or life, go ahead. Be a role model. Trust me, you are enough for yourself.

Live like a badass!

The Notebook

Whenever I am stressed out or overwhelmed with some emotions, I take out my notebook.

This notebook has been my true companion through my ups and downs. When I was in my teens, I was a bit socially awkward. At that time too, this notebook helped me a lot.

There, I blurt out everything that comes to my mind. I feel wanted and heard. And the best thing is the assurance that it would not judge me. I am a free soul here, expressing my feelings without fear.

"Ah! A big relief."

Did you ever blow up a balloon? When you fill the excess of air in it, it bursts. Our mind works the same way. When it is full of thoughts, you feel uncomfortable and restless. A conflict arises in mind and you are often in a dilemma - what to do/what not to. They are the disturbances on the surface of your mind.

Secondly you are unable to share those conflicts with others. If you face the same, then take out your notebook. Jot down all your thoughts. Don't bother about the language, grammar etc. Be you and write what is going on in your mind and heart.

This is the best way to feel lighter.

During my gloomy days, writing became my elixir. It saved me from breaking down. As time went by, I realised one can never be alone if he/she befriends the notebook.

Self-love

Until a few years ago, I did not know the importance of self-love. I had considered it narcissism or arrogance. For me, self-love was selfishness.

However, with time, I realised that self-love is the only means by which one can be selfless. What can you expect from the one who didn't learn to love oneself? Love begins from within. If one fails to love oneself, how can he/she love others?

I realised that I needed to recognize my feelings, and soft desires first to understand others' feelings. The moment I realised it, I promised myself to keep my mental health on top.

And now, I do every possible thing to love myself.

I often fall sick. Though it's frustrating, I keep patience with my body and take care of it by whatever means I can. I stopped mistreating my body with unhealthy food and alcohol. Whenever I get time, I do exercise. At least, a walk for 20 mins.

I make sure that my mental peace remains intact. No matter how close someone is, if my mental peace is affected by being with them, I maintain a distance. Because in the past, I have let myself suffer enough. No more suffering now!

I avoid toxic people and talk only to people who support me and inspire me to do better in life.

I have been short-tempered. Earlier, I got furious if someone did wrong to me. Now, I try my best to forgive people quickly and forget them, because I hate to see the inner me boiling in anger and losing energy. I have forgiven people who hurt me in the past, not because they have changed and become good to me but I have forgiven them for my own mental peace. I got rid of regret, sadness, blame, anger, resentment and the desire for revenge.

I have started working on my dreams as I want to see myself fulfilled. I am trying to avoid procrastination and laziness. They are my enemies, often blocking my way.

I take a stand for myself and speak up if I am criticized by others unnecessarily. I neither scold or berate myself for being fickle nor blame myself for anything unpleasant that happened in the past. I never compare myself with anyone but I accept the inner me wholeheartedly.

I treat myself how I wish to be treated or how I treat others. I am kind to myself and approve of my desires.

I feed good thoughts to my brain by reading books. I feel there is always a need for a teacher who can guide us on how to live in this world. And who can be better than books? So I often buy myself good books.

Where There is a Will, There is a Way

My friend Ashwin tells me about the poverty he had gone through during his student life.

His hometown was a small place where higher education was not possible. He was a bright student and aspired to become successful in life. So he wanted to join a reputed university in a different city.

When he hesitantly expressed his desire to his family, his father was the first person to oppose this idea. He told him that it wouldn't be possible as he wouldn't be able to manage the finances.

Ashwin was dismayed and didn't want to continue this crisis in future as well.

He somehow convinced his father that he so desperately wanted to study further. His father took some loans from an acquaintance and with that money, sent him to the city where he enrolled in college.

That's it! After that, he had to manage almost all the expenses on his own. He provided tuition to children and made some money for survival. Later, he did some interpretation jobs to earn.

At times, he didn't have anything to eat. And the only meal that he could afford was self-cooked Rice, dal and boiled mashed potato.

"Didn't you feel hopeless eating the same food every day?" I asked him.

"I didn't want to continue the same life in future. I wanted to become so rich that I could afford anything that I wanted. So, this food made me adamant to bring change in my life." He retorted.

His zeal, aspirations and adamance worked out. He is a successful entrepreneur now and, in a position, to help others as well. He has helped many people to establish themselves in their life.

While hearing his story, I recalled the great Indian philosopher Swami Vivekananda who made the powerful remark, **"If the mind is intensely eager, everything can be accomplished—mountains can be crumbled into atoms."**

A Beautiful World in the Making

My son had been pestering me to visit the Aero museum for long. Due to time constraints, I was not able to make it.

This time, he had become so adamant that I couldn't put off his demand. So on Sunday afternoon, we decided to visit the museum.

We were out in a cab. The huge traffic was quite frustrating. Though it's quite normal in Bangalore and one can easily have a siesta while travelling even for a short distance, I could never get used to it. The museum is not too far from my house, but looking at the traffic, it seemed like it would take more than one hour to reach. Bangalore's roads are never empty. One cannot enjoy the ride here as much as they can enjoy the beautiful weather of this city. Travelling sucks.

I was engrossed with these thoughts and my child was interrupting every now and then with his countless questions.

Suddenly, he screamed in agony.

"Mumma, Mumma! Please pray to God for that sick person who is in the ambulance", he said folding his hands in a gesture of praying.

I then noticed an ambulance on the opposite road. I couldn't resist hugging him.

"Hurry up, Mumma. You can hug me later also." He sounded anxious.

I nodded and immediately closed my eyes. I prayed for that unseen person, folding my hands and then thanked the universe for moving my child in the right direction.

Years ago, I had once taught him this and explained how the person might be suffering inside the ambulance. We don't go out frequently, so he doesn't get to see an ambulance. Still, he remembered my lesson.

While writing about this incident, I am feeling emotional. I always thought that I would nurture my child differently. He would be full of emotions, compassion and kindness.

I wonder if I am really succeeding.

Sometimes, sitting alone, I imagine a world where everyone has emotional concern for everyone. A world where one's grief can be owned and empathised by others. If we together start instilling this empathy in our children, don't you think we will be able to establish a beautiful world around us?

If we expect others to be kind and generous to us, let's be first kind and generous to them.

Our Assumptions

I would be 6-7 years old. I used to sleep with my parents. In their room, there was a big window close to the bed. While lying in bed, I could see outside.

My father used to have fun with me by telling some funny stories. Mother and I giggled listening to his stories. I think I always slept before them. One such night I was not getting sleep. After some funny, wise talks, my parents fell asleep while I was awake. I looked out through the window and saw something strange in the darkness. A tall, thin man was standing with both hands extended on either side. I got scared and immediately closed my eyes.

After a few minutes, I opened my eyes to check if that man was still there. Gosh! He was still there. This time, he was shaking both of his hands gently.

It frightened me so much that I started crying loudly. My parents woke up and asked me what happened. I pointed out my finger towards the window and told them that there was a ghost outside.

My father looked out to see the man and then took me in his arms. He comforted me and told me that it was not a ghost but a papaya tree. The hands are nothing but its branches which shook as the wind blew.

Later, in the morning, he advised me to not assume but find the facts.

This life-changing advice became my mantra in later years.

In our life, we are trained to assume. And most of the time, we assume negative results which cause fear, worries, nervousness and anxiety.

I well remember my fear when I got the first job offer after completing my studies. I had to shift to Bangalore from New Delhi. I was afraid of not adjusting to the new job profile or the city. I had no idea about the reinsurance domain. I was so frightened of my assumptions that I wanted to reject the offer. However, my brother-in-law gave me the courage to face it and then I joined the second largest reinsurance company in the world.

The same thing happened when I was struggling in my failed marriage. My assumptions were assuring me that I would be in a more miserable situation if I went for divorce. However, I somehow dared to go against my assumptions. And I realised how my assumptions had been misguiding me for years.

In the last three years, many people have advised me to go for remarriage as I would be left alone in my old age. I can appreciate them for their advice, but now, as I am more composed and aware of these pointless assumptions, I can't approve of them.

Who knows if I would be left alone or if I would be leading more fulfilling life than one can think of?

There have been numerous talented people on this planet from time to time but not all of them got the recognition. They could not come into the limelight just because they could not showcase their talent. Their assumptions intensified their fear of being failed or rejected. And so they lived in dark forever.

From my experience, I learned that most of us do not even try to do things that we wish to do. We are trapped by our own negative assumptions and live in fear all our life.

Can we dare to drop these worthless assumptions which are hindering our growth?

Reading Books

Due to time constraints, I am unable to manage time to read books but I immensely feel tempted by them and read whenever I get time.

I am walking in the streets and the roadside vendors are selling books, it becomes arduous for me to avoid them and walk away no matter how busy I am. I forget everything and stop to check all books they have.

Their colourful covers fascinate me.

I often do online window shopping for books and read their reviews.

I personally feel no one can be lonely if one is interested in reading. Books are a great companion.

It opens windows for you to get fresh air. It opens the door and lets you step out so that you can experience the world outside the shell you have been living in for years.

Reading helps you know whether the world outside is smooth, tough or plausible. Whether you can fit into it.

My mother has been an avid reader. After marriage, she lived in a joint family for many years. Many a time, she read books all night and the next day, she cooked for the whole family. I ask her if she didn't feel exhausted managing households after a sleepless night.

"These books carried an air of fascination for me. I couldn't resist completing them in one go." She retorts.

I am not that carefree like my mother. I worry about the consequences of spending time on one thing. Still, these books give me an assurance of being my companion for a lifetime.

A Lesson for Daughters

We are living in the 21st century but the mentality has not changed much for women. In our country, women are still placed as Second Class Citizens. No matter how much we talk about women's empowerment, it will not succeed if we don't start it right from our homes.

So here, I have jotted down some points for Indian parents that they should tell their daughters without fail:

104. Marriage is not the ultimate goal of life. Your studies and career are more important than your marriage.

105. Find a lover in your boyfriend/husband, not your father. Don't compare him with your father, as everyone has a different role to play.

106. Live life with self-esteem. Don't let anyone treat you like cattle.

107. Understand the difference between ego and self-esteem.

108. Your husband's house is your own house but you are always welcome to our house whenever you need us.

109. Be a graceful woman but don't lose yourself in that process.

110. Treat your husband like a king only when he treats you like a queen. Don't be super submissive in the name of an ideal wife.

111. Learn to move on if you are betrayed in a relationship. Shedding tears would not help.

112. Stand for yourself whenever your dignity seems to be in danger. Learn to raise your voice against injustice.

113. Finally yet importantly, Indian parents must introduce pills, condoms and safe sex to their daughters. Those days are gone when the women were confined to four walls. Now, they have more exposure and, in many cases, they have been seen as misguided and lost due to a lack of awareness and moral support that they should have received from their parents.

If we wish to make a better world, let's take a step to become more friendly with our daughters and teach them everything beforehand. This will help them stay strong during their tough times and face the circumstances with courage.

Receptive

Receptive

I fell in love with this word the moment I learned it.

The receptive is the one who is willing to consider or accept new ideas.

You see, there are many people who are too adamant to change. They have developed a belief that the opinion they hold is the only right opinion. Such people never bend. They will never listen to you.

Such people are weak inside, though they look confident. They carry some unknown fear of losing authority which is absolutely worthless and shows their insecurity.

Whenever I read a book, I sideline all my thoughts and beliefs. This helps me understand the writer's thoughts better and accept the ideas without a clash.

And this way I am able to read the book from the writer's perspective. If my thoughts dissent from the thoughts written in the book, without judging the writer, I try to figure out what made him believe/write so. This again helps me to widen my thought process.

Recently, I was reading a book where the writer simplified sex which is still a taboo in our society. According to her, sex is for pleasure and being in love, exploring another body is a divine experience. However, I had a different opinion — why does one always need to offer one's body to prove being in love? But I couldn't go against the writer. We humans are not the same, we have absolutely different mindsets, needs, desires and abilities to execute life. And they can never be completely wrong.

So I love to be receptive. Because this keeps me at ease.

Dear Readers,

I didn't change my life overnight. There was a process that I followed and made sure that I had some discipline to adhere to. Having a disciplined life is much required but it's absolutely okay if you fail in it some days. As every day cannot be the same, you too can miss out on the process and come on track when you feel like coming back.

The only thing you must not forget in this process is your determination. You need to be determined to change no matter even if you have to restart your life completely. You don't have to bother about what others will think of you. Their job is to think, so let them think and your job is to work on yourself and constantly improve, so figure out how you are going to achieve that. Remember, giving up is easy which anyone can do. You are not among those anyones, you are a warrior and you are determined to become a conqueror.

In my diary, I noted down some daily habits that helped me overcome the negativity and have a better life. I would like to share those habits with you, hoping that they help you to change your life:

1. Stop eating the moment you feel your stomach is 80% full.
2. Eat more fruits and vegetables. Avoid eating junk as much as possible.
3. Make a habit of reading a few pages of a book every day.

4. Walk at least for 30 minutes daily.

5. Avoid being sedentary for long hours. Move your body parts every now and then.

6. Talk to people for a few minutes who are positive towards life.

7. Drink 7–8 glasses of water.

8. I talk to the vegetable vendor, domestic help and security guard and ask them about their life whenever I meet them. They feel special and I get attention — both the parties feel happy.

9. Help people whenever you get a chance. This will give you confidence.

10. At times, think negative, something like, what if your parents, spouse, children were not there around, how empty you would feel, or, what if you were jobless, how miserable your life would be. This will give you immense satisfaction and make you grateful for things that you have.

11. Jot down the things in a notebook that you are grateful for in your life. Make it a practice for every day and read them aloud when you get time.

12. Play with children. They are a source of positivity.

13. Smile. Sometimes with no reason.

14. Try to sleep for 6–7 hours every day. This will keep your mental health intact.

15. Grow plants. It will keep you active both mentally and physically.

Meanwhile, I hope all of you will benefit from this book and also from the suggestions listed above. I would be happy to hear from you in this regard. My email address is anshu. ronie@gmail.com

Wishing you all the best!

Anshu Bharti

CPSIA information can be obtained
at www.ICGtesting.com
Printed in the USA
LVHW031548090423
743882LV00020B/277

9 789395 217149